Acknowledgments

These words would never have made it between covers if not for Beth McAuley's unwavering faith and trust in my abilities as a writer and in the worthiness of these stories. She, and her team of editors at The Editing Company, walked me through the whole process, pushing me just enough to meet deadlines and get it written. A word of thanks should go to my sister, Nancy Eyerman, who boxed up all my letters from Europe and sent them up to me. I also need to thank the entire Pak family for giving me an office-away-from-home at the Tik Talk Cafe. Their chicken noodle soup and words of encouragement kept me writing. Thanks need to go to Julie Martine, Olga Sa, Christina Baldwin, Lynda Tam and Vicky Bach for reading various drafts of these stories and giving me their excellent feedback, and to Judith McCaffery, Len Lewis, Renaldo Jo and everyone else who let me talk on and on about my writing. A special thanks to my Social-Media-And-All-Things-Technical Guru, Sarah Wyld, who helped me tip-toe my way into social media and then propelled me by her enthusiasm and organization to stop procrastinating and get the book published. Thank you to Randal Boutilier and his associates at 12thirteen Design, Inc. for the fabulous chapter sketches, cover and production of this book.

And, finally, I want to acknowledge my mother, Margaret Eileen Eyerman, who saved all of my letters from those travels in Europe in the 1970s. She would have been pleased to see this book.

Introduction

In 2006, a year after my mother died, I received a shoebox in the mail. On top was a note from my sister, Nancy. It read: "You should do something with these!" An obligation was definitely implied. Inside the shoebox were all the letters and cards and some souvenirs I had sent my mother during the time I lived around Europe and Northern Africa from 1973 until 1981. Unbeknownst to me, she had saved each and every one of them. My mother knew me well enough to suspect that if she handed them over too early I would have destroyed them, as I had done with some other reminders of my past. And now, here they were, back in my hands.

I didn't open the box right away. Unlike Pandora, I knew there was going to be some unpleasantness in this rediscovery. There were some memories of that time that I would just as soon not be reminded of, so I left the box unopened, and stored it under my bed to age for a few years more. When I finally opened the box and removed the letters, smells, people, addresses, discomforts, vistas, food, languages, the Mediterranean, rooms, landladies and an image of a very shy, skinny, mid-twenties Annie Eyerman came roaring back to me. My mother had given me back memories that I had long since lost. "You should do something with these!" Now I could hear my mother through my sister's words.

I sorted the letters by country and then by date—there were over a hundred of them. (Do any mothers save emails and text messages these days from their traveling offspring?) Some of the letters were sent in cheap gray envelopes (she always saved the envelopes along with their contents), but most were written on those blue aerograms that you could buy at the post office in almost every country. I noticed that I always typed the first letter from each new country so that the return address was as clear as possible for my mother who would most definitely write me back. I put all of the letters into bright-colored folders—a different shade for each country—and left them again. I brought their existence up in conversations with friends as a testimonial to my mother's archival skills. One friend, more persistent than the others, joined my sister's chorus: do something with these! It was time. I finally sat down and reread them, and gleaned the memories that form the basis of these stories. I chose to leave out some of the "facts." I wanted these stories to recapture the experience of living in Europe during the 1970s and to reflect how certain people and events touched *me* and changed *me* during those years.

The Journey

There was no grand plan, no formal itinerary or schedule. Each destination was chosen for a different reason: Dubrovnik because a tour book purported that it was less expensive than Germany; Amalfi for its moderate winter temperature and days of sunshine. I knew people in Villefranche-sur-Saône, Seville and Morroco. Greece just because everyone has to make a pilgrimage to Greece at some point in their lives. And a two-week timeshare got me back to Spain. I would stay in each place for as long as I could. Each country would stamp an entry date and an exit date in my passport when I crossed the border. The rule was that I had to leave the country by or on that specific date. Some places allowed a mere three months; others, more generous with their time, allowed six.

I met some wonderful women on this journey. These are their stories as much as they are mine. Frau Sofia, Kyrie Hermione, Fatima, Suzie and Martha gave me their friendships and recipes. I collected these on loose sheets of paper woven together with kitchen string. I made the cover from the sides of a box of Tide detergent that I bought in Greece and wrote "Cook Book" on it. I still use these recipes, although the "Cook Book" is a bit worn by now. Madame Gravois shared her land and her heritage with me and, finally, Señora Asunción gave me home.

I took some creative liberties with the stories but the people and events are true, as is my experience of them. Thanks to my mother's diligence and pack-rat ways, I can relive those years and bring these stories to you now.

Don't Worry Mom, It's Not a Real Iron Curtain

Dubrovnik, Yugoslavia (Former)

October 1973-January 1974

I am easily intimidated by men in uniforms, especially these two big, green-suited giants who pulled back the door on my train compartment and held out their hands, waiting for me to dig my passport out of my backpack. They were not smiling. To add to the drama, it was the middle of the night, so my groggy self couldn't find the bloody blue book that would tell them I was who I am. I'm always like this at border crossings. I get so nervous I convince myself that I am truly guilty of some crime that even I didn't know I had committed. This nervousness is particularly pronounced when I, a child of the land of liberty and freedom for all, cross behind the dreaded Iron Curtain. Now, heading into Tito's Yugoslavia, I had the same dry-mouth, flip-of-the-stomach fear that I had felt at Checkpoint Charlie two years before, when I was searched for contraband *pfennigs* on the way back from the ballet in East Berlin.

I shamefacedly admit that in 1973 I still carried a silent distrust of Communists. I blame those mandatory Friday-afternoon lectures in grade eight when Father O'Brien would wave his well-thumbed copy of *The Enemy Within* in the air and ask us how we would like it if a Berlin-like wall was built down the middle of Columbus and half of our families were trapped on the other side. I personally thought that would be great if I could choose who to send over, like in a reverse game of Red Rover. But then he'd pull out the big guns and tell us that Communists didn't believe in God. At twelve years old, and with eight years of Catholic schooling behind me, I knew in my heart that I wouldn't want to chance living in a place that didn't believe in God, for heaven's sake.

My mother assumed I was going back to that charming little village in Germany where I'd lived for a year and from which I'd sent her letters full of the aromas of fresh bread and bratwurst. I was pretty sure she would not approve of me crossing into Red Yugoslavia! I thought I could defend my travel destination by appealing to her sense of frugality and pointing out that Germany was now twice as expensive as it had been two years before. I knew her counter reply would be, "You should have stayed in the US of A where you belong," a reply which was to be avoided at all cost. Then I had it. I'd tell her that I had once seen a picture of Marshal Tito, Supreme Leader of Yugoslavia, laughing with her all-time hero, John F. Kennedy (Catholic), while they were sharing conversation or diplomacy or champagne or all three at the White House. Any friend of JFK's was a friend of hers. Then I'd back it up with the fact that Eleanor Roosevelt, also on my mother's list of "good people" (Democrats), had visited Tito at one of his islands. These surely were signs that Mr. Tito was not an archenemy of America and capitalism, so how, I'd argue, could Mr. Tito's homeland be such a bad place for her daughter to go? I didn't think she'd buy it, but it was worth a try.

Meanwhile, back in the compartment, the suspense increased as the green giants left with my passport. They just backed out into the corridor and slid the door closed, leaving me with my mouth open and tears starting to move out of their ducts and into my eyes. To make it all more le Carré-ish, the train started to move, slowly. That was too much and I did what I always do when I am really scared—I dug out my pack of cigarettes and lit one up. But it didn't fool the woman on the other side of the compartment. She knew the truth and finally, to put me at ease, she said in pretty good English, "It is good. We get passports after we cross border." I exhaled deeply to envelop myself in a thick cloud of black smoke while I contemplated this. I wanted to believe her, I did, but it was still dark outside and the whispers of doubt about ever, ever trusting a Communist were seeping into my brain. Then, as if orchestrated to expose my American-made paranoia, the guards came back, smiling now, and handed me my passport with a very official-looking, three-month tourist visa stamped on the first page. My journey had begun.

As the train chugged at what seemed the same laborious pace as the dawn was creeping up over the hills, I watched out the window at the dull, scrub-covered, gray, rocky scenery that did not register high on my beautiful-landscape meter. My perceptive compartment-mate must have sensed my disappointment because she drew me away from the window with words. Her name was Helga and she had studied languages at university. For the past ten years she had been working as a translator in Germany but, alas, she had been called back to take care of her dying mother. I thought it was a toss-up whether her sudden sadness was because of her dying mother or leaving Germany. But as the morning moved into the windows and as the train moved deeper into the rocky landscape of Yugoslavia, Helga, with a sweet, comfortable smile on her face, said, "I am happy to be home." I had the same smile when I had landed in New York after my year in Germany. I didn't want to kiss the ground or anything, but it had been good to be back in a place where I knew I belonged.

Helga waited for me to reciprocate with a story of my own. I dreaded this part. I'm a great listener but can be pretty shy when it comes to talking about myself. I knew I couldn't guarantee not breaking down into sobs if I began with the rotten boyfriend who had broken my heart and dumped me in Munich just before we were supposed to get on this train together. Instead, I told her about my own life in Germany a couple of years before, working in a *Schloss*—the ancestral castle home of some count or another—and traveling to romantic-sounding places like Strasbourg, Vienna and Berlin. I left out the part about being an underpaid, overworked typist/chaperone catering to the whims of spoiled American college students. I did confess, truthfully, that I had fallen in love with European living. Helga nodded. "You are an old soul who needs an old world." I didn't quite know what that meant, but it sounded good.

By the time we reached Split I had totally pushed Helga's evil Communist connections to the far reaches of my mind. As we pulled down suitcases and headed for the door, I knew, for a fact, that Helga would not abandon me until she was sure I was on the right bus for the coast. Outside the train station there was a crowd of babushka-headed women wearing placards and shouting and pulling at everyone who got off the train. All I could make out was the occasional "Room…Cheap." Was this an example of Communist entrepreneurship? Helga explained, "They all have rooms in house to rent, but not enough people to fill them in October." I was very uncomfortable being their main focus of attention. Helga, ever the alert guardian, led me across the street to a red-brick building identified only as "Hotel/Café/Restaurant." I had been warned to never, ever frequent places close to train stations since everyone, except Helga, knew that unsavory types hung out there waiting to prey upon young, single American women. I went in behind her.

Inside was a cavernous, overlit room with not one decoration about it, not even a tiny speck, unless you counted the picture of Favorite Son and Liberator, Mr. Tito. What it did have was an overabundance of harmless-looking, skinny waiters wandering around the empty room straightening not-so-white tablecloths. One of them made his way over to us, bowed, then showed us to a table in the far corner of the room. Why would he maroon us down here, making his trips to and from the kitchen as long as possible? The only thing I could think of was that he must have wanted to make sure this infidel American was as far away from his leader's gaze as possible.

It didn't seem to matter to Helga where we sat. Over cups of sweet, dark coffee and croissants, she mapped out my future. I just listened as she embellished the words from the pamphlets I had picked up in Germany and told me my choice of Dubrovnik was perfect—the weather there was beautiful in the winter and the people more used to tourists. "If my mother was not dying, I go with you." Helga sighed at me. Then, while the skinny waiter listened in, I told her that the most exciting part for me was that I'd be living by the sea. This was a dream that I had tucked into my heart at my first sighting of the Atlantic Ocean one hot August day at Rehoboth Beach in Delaware at the ripe age of twenty. When I finished, she smiled her understanding. "You come to good place. Now you will live your sea dream by getting on bus in Split and off in Dubrovnik." So easy.

By the Sea, By the Sea...

When the bus stopped in the middle of a parking lot, I was worried. Did I miss my stop while I was reading? Ever since the first grade, when the city bus driver forgot to let me off the bus in front of the house until he heard my mother yelling Irish curses at him, I have always been anxious about missing my stop. I didn't know what to do. All the other passengers were shuffling and pulling down their bundles and pushing their way off; even the driver was leaving. I stopped him and showed him my brochure and said, "Dubrovnik?" He grunted something and, since I didn't understand a word, I figured I had a fifty-fifty chance that what he grunted was, "Yes, miss, enjoy your stay in Dubrovnik." So I got off the bus.

I must have lost something in that translation, because when I left the bus there wasn't any sign of a medieval walled city nor St. Blaise, patron saint of stuck fish bones and sore throats, tucked in his grotto protecting the gate. But what was there wasn't bad at all. I was smack dab in the middle of a picture postcard of my idea of paradise (except for the parking lot). There, right in front of me, was the blue, blue Adriatic Sea, just like the brochure promised. What I wasn't expecting were the palm trees, the pine-covered rocky hills, the warm sun and the Technicolor flowers that seemed to pop out of every crack and crevice, even in October. I started to write that first letter to my mom right then and there. I had never been around tropical beauty. I had gone from Ohio to Washington, where I considered the shiny-leafed magnolia tree exotic since it didn't grow in Ohio. Having assumed that all countries behind the Iron Curtain were like East Germany, where everything looked like it was lit by a 40-watt bulb that hadn't been cleaned in a hundred years, I was very happy to put that myth to rest right there and then.

Unfortunately, what was also here was another batch of those babushka-covered, apron-sporting, amply sized Yugoslavian housewives that I had seen in Split, and no St. Helga to protect me. Pushing and smiling my "No. *Nein. Nyet*" through the throng of disappointed landladies, I took shelter in the relative calm of the official Yugoslavian Tourist Office. There seemed to be an unwritten rule that the ladies would not pursue stressed-out tourists beyond these walls. Inside was a young guy whose name plate said "Drazen At Your Service. I Speak English." So I took him up on his offer and asked, "Is this Dubrovnik?" No reply. In fact, he looked at me like I had asked if this was Oz or something. I learned an important lesson: just because someone's name plate says he *speaks* English doesn't necessarily mean that he *understands* English. But something must have gotten through because he brought out a map and pointed at Lapad. "You here," he said. He then traced his finger down the coast line and around a few bends to where St. Blaise and the charming city of Dubrovnik lived.

Disappointment crept into my heart and I asked, "When is the next bus for Dubrovnik?" Drazen ignored me and starting pulling out a selection of full-color brochures showing the attractions of the Lapad Peninsula. There were pine-covered hills stretching down to stony beaches with sea spray I could almost feel, hidden coves perfect for skinny dipping, and more of those palm trees. What more could a girl want for a winter stay? It was beautiful. Drazen must have sensed my interest because he went to another rack and grabbed more propaganda. I had never seen hotels like these; they were built like stairs going down the hills to the sea. I pictured myself sitting on one of those private balconies at sunset, sipping an aperitif and writing to my mother about my luxurious life among the Communists. But my practical side interrupted and reminded me I'd be back in D.C. working a temp-secretary job if I didn't start watching my money. I said to Drazen, "These are very nice but they look too expensive for me." He gave me that open-mouthed stare that I knew meant, "But you're an American, and everyone knows that all Americans are loaded." Later I would find out that all Drazen's ideas about Americans came from old movies and watching *The Untouchables* on television. He asked me once if I knew Eliot Ness. I told him not personally.

I looked out the window at the crowd of my potential landladies and thought about crying, but Drazen sprang into action. "One minute please, lady." I suspected he didn't want a crying tourist on his hands. He started dialing numbers on the phone, then, grinning, he said, "My mother welcomes you." I didn't know whether this meant to Yugoslavia generally or to her home. But as he propelled me towards the door, I guessed it was the latter. Evidently Drazen's mom was one comrade who didn't need to wear a sandwich board at the bus station in order to get tenants. Drazen grabbed my two suitcases, put one of those "Back in five minutes" signs on the door, and then, like my own private Moses, led me through the separating throng outside. I thought this guy should get a raise, if they had such things in a Communist economy.

Drazen led me beyond the palm trees and away from the sea (sigh) and towards those pine-covered hills at the end of the port. Even those seemed exotic to me. It probably had something to do with the clean air and the brilliant light reflected off the sea, or maybe just my lack of sleep. This hill was a whole lot steeper than its sisters had looked in the brochure. I was panting my way up and up, stopping every block to catch my breath while I cursed myself for taking up smoking again. I had righteously quit when I went back to the US, but as soon as I got off the plane in Germany I went looking for one of those cigarette machines that they tucked on the sides of buildings, where you could buy a lovely little five-pack. I falsely convinced myself that I wasn't really smoking again because I didn't buy a full pack. Who was I kidding? I loved smoking, especially when sitting in European cafés by myself, sipping a beer and trying to pretend that I wasn't just a little bit lonesome. So my bad addiction meant that I couldn't run up this hill, so what? I'd get there eventually.

Drazen was waiting for me close to the top in front of a four-floor, modern, very suburban-looking apartment building. I wasn't expecting this at all. My picture of housing behind the Iron Curtain was based on the movie *Ninotchka*, where all the comrades lived in drab, bare apartments that they shared with five other people. They certainly never had balconies and the Adriatic Sea peeking through the pine trees. Another myth destroyed right before my eyes. Drazen held the glass door for me and motioned me up the stairs.

At the top, waiting for us, was my landlady for the next three months. I put on a smile and stuck out my hand and said, "*Guten tag.*" I always pulled out my bad German when meeting anyone whom I suspected didn't speak English. It was the only foreign language I kind of knew and I thought it didn't sound as presumptuous as English. She replied with a smile and a "*Guten tag*" of her own. "*Ich bin Ana.*" "*Ich bin Frau Sofia.*" We had communicated and quite possibly had used up all of our available German vocabulary. I had collected my pathetic supply of German word by word while spending too much time in cafés and *Gausthäuser* drinking wine, eating *kuchen* and gaining forty pounds in one year. I found out later that Frau Sofia learned hers from a German couple who spent one month every year at her house. On every visit they brought her another appliance—vacuum cleaner, coffee maker, electric can opener. Frau Sofia never used any of them but would take them out of their boxes once a year to clean.

I had never lived in the same apartment as my landlady. In Washington, landlords were nothing more than a name on a check once a month or someone to call about backed-up toilets. I wondered how it would be to have one around all the time to see the damage—perceived or otherwise—that I was inflicting on the property. As if reading my doubts, Frau Sofia smiled at me and said, "*Kommen.*" I went. Inside there were four closed doors on a dark hallway; she opened door number one and showed me my prize. I took inventory—twin beds, a built-in desk with the only chair in the room, a closet still full of men's clothes and a picture of mountains and a green valley on the wall in a cheap black frame. I got excited when I saw there was a wall of sliding glass doors, but when I looked out it was over the pine trees and not the sea. This wasn't exactly what I had imagined for my European digs. I thought I'd have something with character, overstuffed, scratchy chairs and pealing walls. I turned to Drazen and asked, "How much?" He turned to his mother and they had an intense conversation that to my thinking took much too long for a simple question like "What's the rent?" When he answered and I figured it in dollars, it turned out to be more than I had paid for my bachelorette in Washington where I didn't share the kitchen, let alone the bathroom. They were waiting. I considered an "*Es kostet zu viel!*" ("It costs too much.") a phrase I had perfected during my latest, very expensive two-week stay in Germany. But then I remembered the women in the plaza and the bag of dirty clothes in my suitcase, so I could only answer, "*Danke, Frau Sofia.*" Home.

Since a deal had been struck, Drazen informed me I'd be having lunch with them that day, a sort of welcome-wagon greeting to my new home. My mother would be impressed with this and pleased that I had found such a good, friendly family to live with, even if they were Communists. Drazen led me into the dining/living/TV room, sat me down at the table and came back with a glass of wine and an ashtray. With a smile he offered me a Marlboro. "It is America," he said proudly. I had always objected to the macho image of Marlboro so had never even tried one. "Thanks," I answered. While we smoked and I drank, Frau Sofia cooked and filled the room with aromas that reminded me I hadn't eaten since that croissant at the hotel in Split. It was good to be home.

Lunch was served when Bruno, the Papa Bear of my new family, arrived. I stood to shake his hand (my mother had taught me good manners) and felt as small as Goldilocks as he engulfed my not-so-small hand into his. Frau Sofia was clicking her tongue, which sent the men of her family and me to the table. Seated, I decided that the best luncheon strategy was to watch the others to see if there was a particular Yugoslavian protocol to eating. However, Frau Sofia gave me no time to pick up any tips. "Frau, *essen*," she said as she shoved the main course towards me. I wished she hadn't done that. I wanted to see how much other people were taking so I'd not appear too greedy, even though my stomach was telling me, "Take more, take more." I slipped the ladle in and came out with one potato, two chunks of meat and some sauce. Frau Sofia looked hurt. I took a second ladle's worth and moved it over to Bruno. When the bread basket arrived, I counted the pieces and divided by four and figured I could take two so I could slurp up the sauce. I ate silently as they chattered away. I was sure that the conversation was all about how fortunate they were to have gotten a sucker to rent their room in the off season. I always imagined the worst when I didn't understand anything. At the end of the meal Bruno got up and came back from the kitchen with a whole head of garlic, which he began to peel carefully, clove by clove, and plunk into his mouth as if it were Belgian chocolate. I watched him from the corner of my eye, not wanting to be included in this particular ritual. I thought myself exotic for cooking with real garlic rather than the kind you shake out of a jar.

I assumed the garlic ritual signaled the end of the meal. I began to gather my German superlatives from the abbreviated lexicon in my head and hoped that Frau Sofia had learned the same words. Then, just when I had the words all in a row, she set in front of me a tiny cup of that sweet, lovely coffee like I had drank in Split. Up until then I had convinced myself that the European blend of Nescafé was an excellent way to wake myself up every morning. Now I'd be thinking about this ambrosia every time I stirred my spoonful of crystals into the boiled water. From the shelf next to the television, Bruno grabbed four little glasses and a bottle whose label identified it as Slivovitz. I had no idea what it was until Drazen offered, "It is brandy from plums." I thought it a tad early in the day to be having brandy, but since I had never had brandy made from plums, or anything else for that matter, what did I know. Drazen and Bruno offered me a cigarette. I had to choose. I thought it might be more politically correct to accept the Yugoslav brand from Bruno. Drazen laughed.

As the plum brandy burned its way down my esophagus, damaging it for life or at least the moment, and as I tried valiantly to not start hacking from these definitely-not-American-mild cigarettes, Drazen gave me my first lesson in Titoconomics 101. "My father is Communist. I am Communist." Was this a trick to confuse the gullible American? Wasn't everyone here a Communist? Or was he was just reminding me that I was living amongst the enemy? But he was smiling. "We are good jobs," he bragged. I had a hard time thinking of jobs like tourist office agent and bank clerk as rewards, but what did I know about the alternatives, so I just shook my head up and down to show him I understood. Drazen didn't mention Frau Sofia, so I guess housewives didn't need to be party members to cook and clean up after the privileged. As I glanced over at Comrade Bruno, I tried to picture those fat, garlic-scented fingers counting out *dinars* behind a teller's window. The image didn't fit the man at all. I found out later that Bruno was really a fisherman at heart. He worked at the bank every day from eight a.m. until one p.m. and after lunch, regardless of the weather, he'd take his little putt-putt boat out and go fishing for cuttlefish that the family used to barter for dry goods and doctor's visits. He never came home empty handed.

Passing the Good Frau Test

The next morning I walked back down the hill for my first venture into grocery shopping Communist style. Drazen and Frau Sofia had spent an hour arguing over which shops they should include on the map I now clutched tightly in my hand. Drazen, being the modern guy that he was, guided me towards the new supermarkets. "Like in America," he bragged. (Drazen equated "good" with anything that came in a package, especially if it came from the home of Al Capone or his hero, Eliot Ness. I had my mother send him a Kellogg's snack pack, which he never ate but put on the shelf next to the Slivovitz to admire and show his friends.) Frau Sofia added her own, bigger marks for the outdoor vegetable market and the spot where the fishing boats came in next to the port. I mouthed the word "Cigarettes?" towards Drazen. He drew an X right at the bottom of the hill. I like convenience in cigarette shopping.

My first stop was, of course, the tobacco kiosk. The woman inside the little round kiosk said, "Good morning." I didn't know if this was a tease or if she really spoke English. "I'd like a pack of cigarettes," I tested her. "Black or blond?" Her hand was hovering over the Marlboros but I said, "Black." Someone had told me once that black cigarettes had fewer chemicals in them, so they wouldn't kill me as fast. She pulled out three packs and laid them on the counter. I recognized Bruno's brand and tapped my choice and asked for matches too. He and I would now be comrades in our smoking pleasure. Although I have to admit that pleasure was not necessarily the word I'd associate with these smokes—rough, cough inducing, foul smelling, cheap. As bad as they were, once I got used to them I was hooked and kept smoking the brand for the full three months of my stay, even after occasionally finding some questionable, definitely-not-tobacco matter inside the white paper. I waved a smiling thank you and she tipped her head at me, knowing I'd be back.

Drazen's supermarket certainly wasn't very "super" in that A&P sort of way. But I kept my American snobbery to myself and pulled out my list of basics: Nescafé, sugar, butter, olive oil, pasta, tomato sauce, laundry detergent and jam. Since I had a surplus of time but not money, I decided to do some comparison shopping between two of the supers. As an interested clerk watched, I began to write down prices to compare with those at the next. I smiled as I left but I don't think she was pleased. At the second, I found exactly the same products and prices, identical to the first. The only variety I found was in the jam section, where, at a considerably lower price, I could buy a jam made from rose hips. I had no idea what those were but guessed they had something to do with the flowering roses on the jar's label. I ate a lot of rose hip jam those three months and never, ever again after that. I loaded my purchases into Frau Sofia's bag and headed for the outdoor market in the parking lot where I had gotten off the bus. Was that just yesterday? Most of the vendors were gone but I was able to find an onion, two potatoes, a slightly wrinkled apple and three carrots in the basket of an old woman who was standing on the corner opposite the market. I liked her spirit of independent entrepreneurship and vowed to shop exclusively at her basket in the future. I was too late for fish. Fish and fishermen wait for no late risers here.

On the way home, I stopped again at the cigarette kiosk for answers. As I approached, the woman looked at me with disbelief that I could have finished that pack of cigarettes already. I smiled and asked, "Are there other places to shop where I could buy different products maybe at lower prices?"

Even my smile did not soften the look of disdain that she gave me. I knew I was in for another lecture on the value of Titoconomics. She proudly told me, "I am not just worker here. I am owner too. It is the same in stores. It is fair that all prices are the same. It makes owners to work hard to have good customers who like us so they will come back and buy more and more so we make more money." I applauded her spirited speech and told her she'd do well in any evil capitalistic society. It made her blush. "I promise to do my part in your enterprise building by smoking lots of these foul cigarettes during the next three months," I told her. It made her smile; she knew I was totally addicted. Then, laden with my vegetarian supper for that night, I climbed back up the hill to home.

I wasn't much of a cook at that time. I could put together a few meals that I had learned by osmosis from my mother. When I first moved away from home at age nineteen, I carried with me only the recipes for my favorite comfort foods—macaroni and cheese made with Velveeta, mashed potatoes and fried dumplings. I had also mastered a few dishes (all of which featured Campbell's soups) to impress my boyfriends; I didn't have enough recipes for a long-term relationship. Since then I had added a few more dishes to my repertoire, including the spaghetti sauce that I was now going to make for my first dinner in Yugoslavia.

I waited until seven to go into the kitchen since I didn't want to bump into Frau Sofia's cooking time. She and Drazen were side by side on the couch staring at subtitles while Dennis Weaver solved a crime on *McCloud*—called *Sheriff of New York* here. I smiled a greeting, not wanting to interrupt their concentration. It felt just like home listening to Dennis's drawl while fixing supper. The kitchen didn't have a door, so I felt rather than saw Frau Sofia's eyes on my back. I kept chopping, thinking that maybe she just wanted to see the American technique for onion cutting. She said something to Drazen, who answered with a grunt. I put the water on for the pasta and splashed olive oil in a skillet. She came closer. As my watched pot refused to boil, she addressed Drazen again, this time with more vehemence. He ignored her. Finally, as if she could resist no longer, she came into the kitchen and motioned for me to go sit at the table. I obliged. She finished my tomato sauce, strained my spaghetti and plated my food. I was mystified. I had no idea what cultural faux pas I had committed, but I was sure it was serious.

The next day I decided to try my hand at fish frying. My kiosk friend had told me I would have to be at the port by seven a.m. to get fresh fish, so I was up at 6:30 and, without coffee or cigarette, headed down the hill to the port. Vegetarianism seemed a tempting alternative at that point. But when in Yugoslavia… I stood with the other women looking down at the boat with the jumping fish and the tired-looking fisherman. Until this moment, the only sardine I had ever seen was lying in oil in a tin can, on which I always cut my finger when I opened it. When it was my turn the fisherman stood up and held a handful of squirming little fish up to my face to show their freshness and, I'm sure, to scare me. I obliged all the ladies and him by letting out a little "Eeek!" I smiled at them, showing what a good sport I was even at this ridiculously early hour. The fisherman was waiting for me so I shook my head yes and he wrapped the little fish in a cone of newspaper and passed them up to me.

As I trudged back up the hill with my catch I felt a tiny twinge of guilt, knowing that the little sardines in my package were still wiggling their last twitch of the tail, sacrificing their lives for my stomach. "I'm sorry" seemed so lame. I should have just stuck to my spaghetti and thrown in some beans for protein. Besides, I had never really liked fish all that much. My brothers used to fish in the creek at night and come home in the early morning with their catch. I'd sit on the back porch and watch them run a knife down the belly of the fish and lop off the heads and throw them to the cat. If I could avoid it, I never ate the fish when my mother cooked it for supper. I'd still remember those little eyes and the smell of guts and blood.

Frau Sofia wasn't home when I got there so I spread the newspaper on the counter and tried to ignore the beady, accusing little almost-alive eyes of the sardines. I told them, "It wasn't me who caught you, after all." Ignoring their silent accusations, I nervously slipped the knife down the belly of the first and gagged as I pulled out the still-warm innards and cut off the heads. One down, eleven more to go. I can't say it got easier, but I did it. By the time I had scaled them and rinsed them off, I only had about half of my catch. I think I did something wrong.

That evening, I was ready for Frau Sofia when I went in to fry my little fish. I gave her and Drazen a "*Guten Abend*" and started to hum "I Have Confidence," not so loudly that it would interrupt the evening news, but loud enough that I could conjure up the image of Julie Andrews twirling her suitcase to get me through my cooking. I put my water on to boil, purposefully slammed a skillet on the stove, poured olive oil into it and got my little plate of sardines out of the fridge. I knew Frau Sofia was right behind me; I ignored her and switched my humming to "When You Walk through a Storm," thinking that with her so close I needed something more substantial. Who knows, maybe she had even seen *The Sound of Music* and would be softened by my humming. She obviously hadn't, because now she was again whining at Drazen, who again ignored her magnificently. She hovered, I watched the pot. I knew enough to know that I shouldn't start frying my fish until my pasta was cooked, but she didn't have my patience. She pushed me aside, again, turned off my pasta water, put my little sardines in the hot olive oil, sprinkled them with salt and chopped-up tomatoes and lettuce for a salad and sent me to the table. Defeat.

The next morning I went to the woman at the cigarette kiosk for some explanations. She was becoming my expert on all things Yugoslav. When I told her what was happening, she rolled her eyes and shook her head at me like I was an enemy of the state. I knew a lecture was coming. She explained, pointing a finger at the wires overhead, that electricity is a precious commodity. This summer there was little rain, so there was less electricity now. So the State in its wisdom had declared that at certain times of the day electricity would be more expensive. Good comrades now do their cooking in the afternoon when it costs less, not at seven o'clock in the evening! She looked disappointed in me, as if I should have figured it out myself. I now felt stupid as well as guilty. "This is not America," she was frowning now. "We work together to make all good." That afternoon I crept into the kitchen at three o'clock. Frau Sofia was there washing windows. I gave her a "*Guten Tag*" and set about cleaning yet more fish, boiled my pasta water in peace, chopped up carrots and steamed them over the boiling water. I felt like a good and righteous comrade in my economical use of electricity. Frau Sofia said nothing as I wrapped everything up and put it in the refrigerator for reheating. That night I was invited to rejoin the family in TV land.

Frau Sofia and I worked out an afternoon kitchen schedule without ever negotiating the terms. She was always first, so if she decided to cook something elaborate, my cooking time would be shortened. I'd have to whip through my preparations like I was playing a game of Beat the Clock, which I was. One day she surprised me by inviting me into the kitchen while she cooked *Grah*. I took this recipe exchange as the first step towards a total dismantling of our own private Iron Curtain. My mother would approve of *Grah*. It was a high-octane bean soup with sausages, potatoes and carrots, thickened with a mix of flour, paprika and olive oil, and it was very inexpensive to make. It was stick-to-your-bones, gas-inducing, wonderful stuff, and the first of many basic peasant dishes that I would come to know and love all through my journey. These are the dishes that you knew were originally put together by poor women who had to feed a brood of hungry kids. My mother was a master at those dishes, which she usually cooked in a big, dented soup cauldron recycled from the cafeteria at St. James the Less. She would make pots of chili, soup beans with bacon grease, ham and green beans, and corned beef and cabbage. (Later in my stay Frau Sofia would show me other dishes in her repertoire that she figured I could manage: cabbage sautéed with garlic and olive oil and mixed with mashed potatoes [my favorite comfort food]; a bigger white fish [with bigger bones and more guts] cooked with cabbage and tomatoes and potatoes in the oven.)

By the end of my second week I had mastered early-rising, cost-saving measures for cooking, learned how to scale fish, learned preliminary lessons in Titoism and added more recipes to my cooking repertoire than I had in the past five years. It was time to reward myself with an escape from the suburbs.

So This Is Where They Keep the Good Stuff

I told my kiosk friend that I was finally going into Dubrovnik. She said, "You need book," and moved cartons of cigarettes and old magazines from under the counter. She came up with a book and handed it to me. The cover was so faded that the blue of the sea was now as grey as the stones in the wall. "It looks pretty old," I said. She replied, "Nothing change. It is English." I looked inside; there were indeed English words, but the sentences read like a bad parody of the language. Maybe I could pick up a job as a proofreader while I was here, but I'm sure a job of that caliber would have to be held by a Communist and I knew for a fact that my mother would disown me if I joined the Party, no matter how prestigious the job. My kiosk friend was waiting. I decided that no matter how faded the book was, it would at least give me an idea of what I'd be looking at, so I paid her. She nodded her head and repeated, "It is English."

This time when I got off the bus I knew I was in the right place, because there in front of me was that walled city with the statue of St. Blaise tucked above its gate. I felt a tiny pang of regret that I had not continued on and settled here within a genuine medieval city. How cool would that be? But, I argued, if I had done that I might never have learned how to scale fish or cook *Grah*. I wasn't convinced by my argument. I decided to start my tour with St. Blaise so I could send up prayers to him to protect me from death by choking, stuck fish bones and strep throat. Amen. But before I could move in his direction, something made me stop and look up, up, up to the hill towering over the plaza, the sea, the town and everything else in a five-mile radius. There, spread out across the top in whitewashed boulders, was a Hollywood-worthy sign with just one name: T-I-T-O. I was impressed and immediately got the message that I, anyone on land, sea or air, and especially St. Blaise should be clear about who was the government-approved, almighty protector of this city.

With tour book tucked under my arm I crossed the drawbridge, went through the gate and down into the city. That first time, and every other time I walked into Dubrovnik, I was awestruck by the almost marble-like white stone streets. I guess that's what can happen when you start out with big slabs of stone, get millions of feet to shuffle over them for centuries and then ban motor vehicles from driving on them. I didn't think it would catch on in America, where it would be considered suspect to ban cars from anywhere. I headed for the stairs to the top of the wall, since that's where the guidebook insisted I begin, and who was I to argue. The steps were crumbling and the drops down on the land side nauseated me, but once I got to the middle with the sea on one side and the red-tiled roofs of the city down below me, I was smitten. Here I was, Annie from Ohio, looking out onto the Adriatic Sea where Venetian merchants, Saracen marauders, holy Crusaders, a lot of sailors and my fisherman landlord, Bruno, sailed. I got all choked up just thinking about it. Do people who grow up by the sea feel this sense of wonder? I kept stopping and looking and stopping and looking so that it took me three times longer to get to the port gate than the book said it should take. I didn't care and was sure that no one would tell them.

It was time to tour the main street of Dubrovnik. Then I remembered: I *lived* here, so technically I was not a tourist and did not have to see everything in one day. (Actually, in my whole three months in Dubrovnik, I never met, ran into or overheard another tourist.) So I went instead in search of a café to have one of those paradise-in-a-cup coffees. As I walked down the marble main street looking for the right spot, I saw it. I wasn't sure if I had really seen it or had only wished it to be there. So I closed my eyes and opened them again to confirm that I had indeed seen, brazenly hanging on a rack outside a newsstand as if it were in Paris, the *International Herald Tribune*! I could not believe it. I was giddy just thinking that by passing some *dinars* over the counter I could, once again, be reading the news from America, classifieds for villas in the south of France and even the scores for Ohio State football! I didn't hesitate, even when I saw that the price was equivalent to several kilos of sardines. This was a necessity. It was important that I keep abreast of what was happening in the world, wasn't it? Whether it was or not, I vowed to come into the city each week for a new edition. Now, all I had to do was find a café.

Another advantage of a car-free city was that café tables could be plunked down right in the middle of the street. I always enjoyed taking over streets, so I sat down at one of three tables on the sunny side of the plaza and gave my order to a hovering waiter. When I finally had the coffee, I opened the paper. I wanted to cry at the English words that brought the familiarity of home back to me. I was so engrossed in my nostalgia that I didn't notice my puddle of sun had dried up. There, bowing to me, was a short, older man in a beret and black overcoat. He looked official and I felt guilty. "Good afternoon, miss," he said. My paper was a dead giveaway of my language preference. "You are visiting Dubrovnik?" Should I have brought my passport with the visa all properly stamped to prove I was legit? "Yes." Did my voice really squeak? He asked, "May I join you?" How could I say no? As he sat, he smiled and nodded down at the front page. "You do know that you would not be able to buy that in Moscow?" Since I wasn't in Moscow and had no plans to go I didn't really get his point. He didn't leave me time to ponder: "In Tito's Yugoslavia we are not afraid of ideas. Our people get all the news from the West and from Moscow. It makes us better citizens." With that proclamation, he stood up, bowed, took my hand, kissed it and smiled a goodbye. I knew I had just received another important lesson in Tito Communism. I was beginning to feel like those women in the plaza with their signs reading "Room...Cheap," except mine read, "Ignorant American. Needs Education in Tito Communism. Please Help."

After digesting my most recent lesson, I went back to my reading. Since I knew I wanted this paper to last me the whole week, I decided I would limit my café pleasure to just reading the articles on the front page, not even going to their "continued on page 3" endings. It was a good decision, since the waiter came out at that point and started stacking the other tables and chairs and eyeing me. I packed up and asked him where the restroom was, since I knew I wouldn't make it back to suburbia without first visiting the facilities. He pointed down the street to a little whitewashed building. Had I used the wrong word and asked him instead for a place to buy aspirin or sewing thread? I didn't want to risk another lecture, so I just paid him and made my way down the street. I knew he was watching. When I got to the building, I looked back and he waved me in. There was a narrow porch outside with a chair and a small table with an embroidered cloth. I thought it was pretty considerate of them to have a cushion-covered chair where you could wait if it was occupied. I went in and came out thankful that I always carried tissues in my pocket, since there was no paper in the stall.

As I walked down the street, I was feeling pretty good about my first visit to Dubrovnik and especially about having that *Herald Trib* tucked in my bag. I heard screaming coming from the direction of that whitewashed building. I kept walking and had almost made it to the main street when I felt my ponytail being yanked. Behind me was a short, stocky, apron-clad woman pointing a finger at me and then back to the building. I didn't understand. She kept pulling me backwards until we were in front of that embroidery-covered table. I honestly hadn't seen the little saucer that she was now tapping with authority. I can be pretty dense sometimes, but if I had seen a saucer I may have figured out that you had to pay something to use the toilet. She waited, arms now akimbo, but nervously watching me in case I made a run for it. I knew my face was getting red as other people stopped to find out what was going on. I dug in my purse and put some coins down on the saucer. She smirked at me so I put more. Once again, I felt stupid and shamed. When would all these lessons end? I wasn't really trying to cheat the Communist system, I just didn't know. I suspected that my cigarette kiosk teacher would be disappointed in me. She had already given me the lesson on the worker/owner arrangement, and here I was, penalizing this woman's chance to maybe show a profit this month or earn commendation from the Party leaders. On the bus home, I decided it was better not to tell my kiosk comrade about my failure to remember her lessons, just in case she refused to sell me any more of those foul cigarettes.

Going Home...Or at Least Someone's Home

While I may have been forgetting my lessons on workers' rights, I must have passed the test on the home front, because Frau Sofia invited me to go with her to visit her brother who lived in the Konavle Valley, which, according to my faded-covered tour book, was full of mountains, cypress trees and grapevines. It sounded divine. But it also said that it was located some twelve miles from Dubrovnik, and that seemed a long distance to travel with someone who did not approve of my smoking and with whom I could only communicate with smiles, head nods and our minuscule collection of German words. I hesitated accepting and then, like getting a telepathic message from Ohio, I heard my mother's voice saying, "Oh Annie, go, wear something nice and watch your manners." She was usually right.

In the spirit of traveling light, I hadn't brought any of my out-to impress clothes, so the best I could do for "nice" was putting on my most unfaded pair of corduroys, a turtleneck and a hand-knitted vest that was a discard from one of the students in the *Schloss*. I thought I looked pretty good until I saw Frau Sofia, who was dressed in a tight-fitting black V-neck dress, heels, makeup and a slight bouffant flip to her hair. I gave her a short whistle and said, "*Sehr gut!*" She didn't return the compliment.

As we headed down the hill to catch the bus into Dubrovnik, Frau Sofia kept shifting the bouquet of flowers she was carrying from one arm to the other. I didn't know the word for "carry" in German so I just made the motion, which looked an awful lot like rocking a baby. She said "*Nein, danke,*" which was nice. I was feeling happy and wanted to sing something jaunty, but the only thing that came to mind was that old German hiking song, "*Falleri, fallera, falleri, fallera ha ha ha ha ha*" and it was too early in the morning for that. Frau Sofia didn't even comment when I stopped at my kiosk to buy cigarettes, but just waited for me on the other side of the street. As I pulled out change I told my kiosk comrade in an excited voice, "I'm going to the Konavle Valley." She looked at me with a serious face and I knew I was about to get a lecture on the contributions of the agricultural workers to the common good. Fortunately for me, Frau Sofia was calling "*Schnell.*" The lecture would have to come later.

When we arrived at the bus plaza in Dubrovnik, there were at least a dozen other black-clad, flower-bearing women standing around waiting for the bus. Frau Sofia linked her arm in mine and walked towards them. I knew I was about to become the main feature of her show-and-tell. I sent a silent prayer over to St. Blaise to protect my shy self from what was about to happen and, to cover all my bases, also threw words of the same ilk up to T-I-T-O, but left off the "Amen," of course. The ladies gathered around us and Frau Sofia beamed and pointed at me. They all looked me over and I apologized silently to my mother for the corduroys. Then I heard the word *Američki* and imagined an exclamation point behind it and waited for another lecture, or at least for them all to move away from me like a plague. But all I got were smiles and handshakes. Frau Sofia started pushing me onto the next bus and into the first seat next to the driver like it was an honor. I didn't tell her that I hated this seat because there is no way to avoid watching the road and all the death-defying, stupid maneuvers the driver makes. I would just close my eyes.

As soon as the bus started up, the party began. Not one of those women sat down, but moved around the bus passing out candies and cookies and I'm sure talking about anything but husbands and cleaning. Every once in a while the driver would turn around and shout something back at them, which was received with uproarious laughter; then one of the women would throw words right back at him. It had that delicious, universal, not-serious, sexual feel of flirting that always happens when women are free from daily chores and together with friends and a "safe" man. It reminded me of being out with my married sisters when they'd have a drink with lunch, bum one of my cigarettes and flirt with the waiter.

When Frau Sofia and I got off the bus, the view was just what the tour book had promised: cypress trees, grapevines, olive trees and plowed fields stretched across the valley. It was stupendous and in more brilliant shades than the monochrome picture in the book. I started to imagine living out here, having a little garden, stomping grapes for wine, putting up tomatoes for the winter. But this planning of my agrarian life had to be quick, since Frau Sofia was already hiking up her good black dress and climbing over the fence. I was impressed that she managed to do that without running her hose or dropping the flowers. It was my turn. As she waited, I clumsily hauled myself up and over that fence, landing with a plunk near her feet. She was smiling but I wasn't sure if it was because of my awkward ascent/descent of the fence, or because she, like Helga, was home.

We walked along a rocky path, under olive trees and around plowed fields, until we reached a tiny graveyard plunked in the middle of everything. This wasn't one of those Happy Acres kinds of resting places; this one had felt the wind and rain of centuries. There was a waist-high stone wall with big chunks taken out of it and never put back. At one end was a narrow wooden gate with a carved cross on the top. Frau Sofia pushed her way through and tiptoed, like she was in church, between the headstones. She stopped at the first grave in the last row and started brushing furiously at every leaf, twig and rotten olive that had fallen there in the last year. I stooped down to help her and saw that the people buried here had died in the 1930s. I wondered if it was during the Second World War, when Tito was up in the mountains trying to liberate them. I looked around and saw that other graves had also been cleaned off and fresh flowers put on them. Then I remembered it was November 1, All Saints' Day, when all good Catholics (and probably Anglicans too) go to the cemetery to remember their dead. That's why the ladies were all in black and why they had those flowers. I should have dressed better, or at least worn black. With the cleaning finished, Frau Sofia and I knelt down and almost simultaneously made the sign of the cross. I looked at her and she at me in a way that said that with all our differences, we were the same in this outward sign of faith. As Frau Sofia cried for the people buried there, I said my own prayers for my grandparents I had never known, for my Uncle Tom who was the first and only dead person I ever saw and for all the souls who didn't have anyone else to pray for them. When we got up to leave, I knew I had just received another lesson in Tito Communism. Here, a Frau Sofia living with two Communists was still free to believe in her God and even say a few prayers.

As soon as we were out the gate, I knew that it was going to be a slow march across the valley to her brother's. I really didn't mind her wanting to show off her Američki to her friends at home. I was even a little flattered. But after the third house, my mouth muscles were starting to atrophy in a permanent smile and I knew I couldn't eat one more cookie. Frau Sofia pointed me towards a fire escape ladder that hung on the side of whitewashed farmhouse. I have always been a little leery of climbing stairs that you can see through, but she was right behind me, so I had no choice but to move on up. The reward at the top was wonderful. She had saved the best for last. The terrace overlooked the entire valley and the mountains and was filled with pots of blooming geraniums (my mother would be jealous), two beautiful kids and an old woman dressed in the traditional long black skirt with a bright blue apron, white blouse and a sash of yellow and gold embroidery just like I had seen in the brochures in the tourist office. I was truly with "real people." Frau Sofia handed out her gifts from the city and the old lady gave us coffee and more cookies, which I had to eat, and then we were off. Frau Sofia took the lead down the ladder and I followed, looking straight ahead as I climbed down, taking one rung at a time. By the time I got to the bottom, she was out in a field picking tomatoes and peppers that were still on the plants even in November. I guess this didn't count as stealing if you lived here; I picked only a few, since I was a guest.

Finally we arrived to where her brother and his wife lived and farmed. After hugs and introductions, not that I needed one, Frau Sofia and her sister-in-law went into the kitchen to fix lunch. I wanted to go out and help but they said no, I should stay here and rest. I would have rather gone out and chopped and stirred with the women. That left just the brother, who didn't speak any German—bad or otherwise—so while the ladies were in the kitchen fixing lunch, all I could do was smile and offer him cigarettes and have him return the favor to me. I'm sure we smoked a pack between us by the time Frau Sofia and her sister-in-law came out from the kitchen carrying platters of food. I would write my mother the whole menu: hot fresh greens cooked with potatoes with a hint of bacon grease, smoked meat, cheese, olives, a salad, homemade wine and the best bread I have ever eaten. I prayed to all the saints for their blessing on this house as I shared this meal. After coffee and cookies and a sip of Slivovitz, it was time for Frau Sofia and I to walk back to the road to catch the bus. I noticed that on the way back there was no bantering with the driver or sweets passed around. Maybe all the women were thinking about the month and a half they'd have to wait for Christmas and another visit home.

Knowing When It's Time to Leave

In the weeks following the trip to Konavle, Frau Sofia and I lived in harmony. We weren't as close as we had been, kneeling beside each other in that cemetery, but that was fine. Occasionally hostilities would erupt, usually caused by my foul-smelling cigarettes or, more often, my perceived messiness coming up against her whisk broom. These were the times when I knew our own version of the Cold War was still alive and well. Only once did it almost escalate into our very own Bay of Pigs. I was sitting innocently at the table, having my breakfast of fresh bread and mediocre Nescafé when, armed with a whisk broom and dustpan, Frau Sofia got down on her hands and knees and climbed under the table. She had to know I was still sitting there, but I nudged her with my knee just to remind her. She whisked more forcefully and let out a "*Viele schmudzig*" while bumping my foot to make sure I understood she was talking about me. The confrontation escalated when I swept a few crumbs off the table to the floor in retaliation. She whisked more ferociously, including my feet in her swishes. I wanted to get down there and tell her, with pointed finger in her face, that I wasn't really a dirty person and that I knew the rules for good housecleaning. I had, after all, been cleaning house since I was ten years old when, every Saturday, we six girls would be charged with taking the chaos of a week of fourteen people living in too small a space and making clean order out of it. We were miracle workers. So I was sure I could handle cleaning up after my breakfast and keeping my one small room in good order. Righteousness stirred in me and made me feel that this was about something more important than just my crumbs and her whisk broom. I was defending democracy and possibly liberty and justice for all. Luckily, before I brought our world to the brink of no return, I remembered my mother saying, numerous times, "That hot head and big mouth of yours will get you in trouble some day." She was right…again. I knew I had to keep silent, especially since I had another month to live here. I backed away from the confrontation and from the table, washed my dishes and went for a walk. After that, I let her whisk whenever she wanted.

Another electricity crisis was declared in early December, but this time I had fair warning from my cigarette comrade. "No electricity from seven morning to seven night. We must save for emergency." I thought having heat, hot water and somewhere to cook my *Grah* were pretty essential services but, not wanting to sound like the pampered American again and laying myself open for another lecture, I kept quiet. Our household had been well prepared for the crisis, or at least the no-heat part. All winter Frau Sofia had been keeping the thermostat very close to off. When any of us complained she, like Scrooge, would tell us to put on another sweater or to stop sitting around and get up and do some work that would warm us up. To add to the drama, everyone in the house agreed that this winter was the coldest that anyone could remember. When they mentioned this they always looked my way like I had some kind of weather-controlling powers. Then it snowed for the first time in twenty-five years or maybe even a century, which cast more suspicions on me. It wasn't a big snowstorm, so when Drazen moaned about having to go out, I told him smugly, "When I was a kid in Ohio, I used to walk a mile to school in snow up to my waist." I exaggerated; it was only up my knees, and I was very short. He was properly impressed, but my story meant that I couldn't ask him to pick up my cigarettes for me when he went down to work.

Snow I can deal with even without boots, but overnight there had been a freezing rain storm, so now there was sheer ice over the hill that separated me, cigarette-less, and the kiosk. I thought that maybe this was a good time to quit? I put on my coat and started down the stairs. As soon as I stepped off the porch, I slipped. This was not good. I shuffled down the entrance to the hill. If I wasn't concentrating so hard on not falling, I could have appreciated how beautiful the pine trees looked and the icy gray of the Adriatic. But that was not on my radar. I had to figure out how to maneuver this hill. Was it steeper than it had been two days ago or was it the ice daring me to just try to walk down? I saw no other alternative, so I just sat down right on the sidewalk and used my feet to guide me down the hill right to the base of the kiosk. My cigarette seller was not surprised to see me. She, having heard the weather report, had four packs ready for me. Then she asked, "How do you go up hill?" I hadn't thought of that as I lit up a cigarette to put off the trek home. I smiled at her and asked, "Could I stay here with you?" She smirked and fanned her hand out and around the tiny cubicle of space she worked in. I had no choice but to slide myself over to the hill and then cling to branches and dead plants to pull myself uphill home. Of course, at home there was no heat, no hot tea, no warm anything. It took two hours under the covers, four pair of socks and too many of those cigarettes to start to thaw out. I heard my mother tsking at me, "You'd risk dying of pneumonia for cigarettes?" I turned her voice off.

After two weeks, the electricity came back. I never knew whether it was because we had all been such good comrades or because the women of the town said "Enough is enough, we have baking to do" that disaster was averted. Whatever it was, the week before Christmas the switch was pulled and we had light. Frau Sofia must have been feeling the holiday spirit, because she even turned the heat up so we could all shed one layer of clothes. One afternoon I went to the dining/living/TV room, pretending to read but really just wanting to hang out around the kitchen so I could smell all the cookies and cakes Frau Sofia was baking. It felt just like my mother's kitchen and I was immediately homesick. Frau Sofia sensed my sadness and came over with one of those paradise-in-a-cup coffees and some samples of all her baking. I knew at that point that there would be no whisking around me from now until after the holidays.

That week when I went into Dubrovnik for my *Herald Trib*, I noticed that shop windows were more festive. There wasn't a Santa Claus to be seen, and certainly no nativity scenes, but it still had that feeling of goodwill and buy-buy-buy. I am a sucker for Christmas, so I looked in every window on the main street until I found a tiny jewelry store across from the newsstand. I decided to go in and buy myself a birthday present, since no one else would. I can become quite maudlin about the wrong that was done to me by being born on Christmas Eve and all the years of neglect. But that approach never made me feel better, so a couple of years ago I had decided to just buy myself a gift, wrap it up, sing "Happy Birthday" and tell myself how much I liked it. I've gotten some of my favorite gifts that way. This year it would be a silver necklace with a filigreed pendant with a green stone in the center. I'm sure it was made for the tourist trade, but I didn't care. It said Happy Birthday just fine to me.

When I got home Frau Sofia called me out to the kitchen for another cooking lesson. This time it was cabbage rolls. I had never even eaten a cabbage roll, let alone made one. Anyway, the cabbage smells coming out of that kitchen reminded me an awful lot of sauerkraut, which falls even lower than liver on my least-favorite-foods list. Frau Sofia was not interested in my likes one way or the other. "*Bitte, machen*," she said. She pointed to her eye and then to me and said, "*Kuck' mal!*" It definitely sounded like an order, so I watched. She put a cabbage leaf the size of a dinner plate on the kitchen counter, then added a dollop of stuffing (I found out later it was a mix of ground pork, onions, garlic and spices). She folded that leaf into the tightest, most perfect cabbage roll I'd ever seen—not that I'm an expert. Now it was my turn. This did not seem difficult at all. I placed the leaf down; she watched. I then plopped a spoonful of filling in the center; she grunted something and threw in a bit more. Now I had to fold. It was a lot more difficult than it had looked when she did it. My cabbage roll turned out slightly lopsided and in danger of falling apart if anyone touched it. She raised her eyebrows; I unfolded it and started over. By my fourth try I had it and she allowed me to tuck my almost-perfect one in the big roasting pan with hers. Then she poured a tomato sauce over the whole thing and plunked a big glob of some kind of animal fat in with it and cooked it slowly in the oven for hours. Having lived through two electricity crises in just two months, I marveled at her reckless disregard for how many kilowatts she was using. I guess that's what the holidays are for no matter where you are.

On the twenty-fourth I opened my gift to myself and decided not to leave my room all day. I didn't want to risk getting weepy and have someone ask me why. I had tangerines, a loaf of bread, pâté and another bottle of that sour wine to drink a toast to myself later. Then the door opened and there were Frau Sofia and Drazen shouting "Happy Birthday," or I think that's what they said. Drazen looked smug and said, "I see passport. I am good detective." Since my passport was, I thought, locked away in the desk drawer, I wondered what else he had discovered. But I wasn't about to complain because he was leading me like an honored guest into the dining/living/TV room, where Frau Sofia had set out a breakfast worthy of home. Drazen boasted, "It is American breakfast. I see on TV." Then Olga, who lived across the hall, came in and gave me a plate of hot Berliners, those lovely fried doughnuts with a squirt of jam inside (definitely not rose hip). We all sat down with paradise-in-a-cup coffees and ate all the Berliners right then and there. It was a good birthday.

That night Frau Sofia and I went to Dubrovnik for midnight mass. We went to the church at the Franciscan monastery that was tucked into a corner of the wall close to the port. The place was packed, which surprised me in this Communist country, but by that time I should have learned all the ways that this Communism was different from the others. I was silently thankful for the years of participating in this Catholic tradition, which gave me the inside scoop on what all this mumble-jumble was about, no matter the language. It was a folk mass complete with two fiddles, a banjo, a piano, a mandolin and a bass. I was waiting for them to start "Kumbaya" at any moment, but instead they went into a four-part harmony of "Silent Night". I cried and felt more homesick than I had for a long time.

On New Year's Eve, when all good Communists start their holiday celebrations, Olga the Berliner-bearing neighbor included me in the invitation to her home. When I walked in I thought about asking her if I could spend the rest of my time, maybe my life even, at her apartment—it was that comfortable. There was good art on the walls, sofas stuffed with pillows, lamplight, oriental carpets, a Christmas tree and chaos. It was as warm and messy as Frau Sofia's was neat. She introduced me to her gorgeous husband, who was just back from conducting the Vienna Philharmonic. Before I got my tongue-tied thoughts in line to tell him about my own trip to Vienna, not to conduct the orchestra, of course, he was giving me what would be my final lesson in Communism à la Tito. "Here, you have a clerk in the bank and an orchestra conductor as neighbors and friends living in the same apartment block. Would you find that in Vienna or New York?" I told him I couldn't imagine Leonard Bernstein living next to anyone in my working-class family. He then handed me a flute of champagne and everyone shouted *"Stretna Nova Godina."* As we danced in 1974, I didn't even miss Guy Lombardo and the dropping ball.

A few days later it was time to leave. Frau Sofia helped me do my laundry and clean the room so that Drazen could move back in when I left. That last week I ate all my meals with the family and only went to the market to say goodbye to the fisherman and the old lady selling potatoes. I gave my kiosk friend a copy of John Steinbeck's *Journal of a Novel* that I had surprisingly found at the newsstand one day in Dubrovnik. I thought she might appreciate reading a little about America, just in case she decided to take her business acumen to the other side of the world. She gave me a postcard of the Konavle Valley as a going-away gift. The whole family walked me to the ferry that would take me across the sea to Bari, Italy. The boat left at midnight on the last day of my visa, so it seemed appropriate to have the people I had met at the beginning of my stay here at the ending. Frau Sofia even linked her arm in mine like the friends we had seemingly become, and I almost forgot all about her whisk broom.

I don't like goodbyes ever, so after hugging each one of them I got aboard the boat, even though it wouldn't leave for another half hour. When I was sure they were gone, I went out on the deck because this would be my virgin voyage on any sea and I didn't want to miss one second of it, except maybe the nausea from the rocking boat. I lit up a cigarette and thought about all the good lessons I had been taught in Tito Communism, and what Father O'Brien would say to all that.

That's Amore?

Amalfi, Italy
January–April 1974

Getting to Domani

I met Suzie on my first day in Amalfi. I had just gotten off the bus and put my two mismatched suitcases down, one on either side of me, when a red Volkswagen bug came roaring by right through the ill-fated puddle in front of me. I was now dripping. There was no room for another drop to be absorbed by my clothes, since they were already drenched from standing at the bus stop for an hour. It wasn't supposed to rain in Italy, at least not according to my guidebook and every movie made in Italy that I had ever seen. I mean, really, did Sophia Loren ever have to dodge puddles? Did the girls in *Three Coins in the Fountain* have to carry an umbrella? Never. Italy was supposed to be all sun and sexiness and right now I had neither. I wanted to shake a fist and send curses up to some god or other, but I couldn't remember which ones were Roman and which Greek, and didn't think it was such a good idea to stir up any jealous pride.

This splasher of innocents was now getting out of the car and making her way to my dripping self. "I am so sorry. I didn't see you there. Are you ok?" I do have a problem with invisibility sometimes, but I *was* the only person standing on the side of the road. "Come on. Let's go get a coffee. My treat." What could I say? She was already across the street with my two suitcases and tilting her head towards a little café. I followed. I adore almost everything about Italy, except for the fact that you have to stand up to drink your coffee at the café bars. This one was no different. It was in a tiny, narrow building across from the town's Cathedral. One whole wall was windows, so you could lean an elbow on the zinc bar that stretched from wall to wall, sip your coffee and never miss a thing that was happening in the piazza outside. When we walked in everyone at the bar, all men of course, said in unison, "*Ciao,* Suzie." She was a regular. As she shrugged off her jacket to reveal a V-neck white angora sweater filled with very ample breasts, I understood all the attention. Suzie was everything I was not—blond, voluptuous, dry and, as I would soon find out, liberated. She bestowed smiles on each of the men in turn and then flirted just enough with the waiter to get us a coffee and a space at the bar.

I am a real admirer of anyone who knows how to flirt and, even though I didn't know Italian, I knew Suzie was a pro. I've always been too shy to really do it well but I had a feeling that in the next three months I was going to learn a thing or two about flirting from this Suzie-Q. As we lit cigarettes and gulped the tiny espressos, I told her my story of heartbreak and abandonment in Germany. She gave the usual, "Men are bastards," then followed up with a pat on the hand and "Well, it's always better to be a single woman when in Italy." I wasn't sure I agreed, having read about pinched bottoms.

Suzie's story took another coffee and a good many more cigarettes. She had been working as a secretary at Yale University, helping overpaid and arrogant academics get research grants that would send them to Europe while she sat in New Haven. "Last summer I declared, that's enough. It was my turn." So she signed up for Italian lessons, saved her money, dipped into a trust fund her grandfather had left her and in the fall headed for Amalfi. "I'm not ever going back," she declared with bravado. Then, with perfect timing to create the maximum reaction, she said, "I came to Amalfi for the explicit reason to have as many affairs with as many Italian men as I can handle before I turn thirty. I have four years to go." She laughed just enough to take what must have been a shocked look off my face. "I figured coming in the winter would limit the competition," she added. I wanted to ask her how it was going, but thought it would have sounded like asking her how many notches she had on her gun. Anyway, I figured she'd tell me at some point. How could anyone keep such juicy information to themselves, especially an American woman?

Whether any of it was true or not, I loved the daringness of her plan. It made me wish, yet again, that I was able to free myself enough to really enjoy this sexual revolution. I had, of course, dipped my toes in the waters, but it was always with much guilt and shame. I had always wanted love and romance first and then sex, which was way out of step with the sexual revolution of the 1970s. Suzie's plan reminded me of my friend Trudy in Washington, who would brag to me (I'm sure to point out my own lack of sexual prowess), "I like to walk through Dupont Circle at lunchtime and pick up one lover and then meet the next one in the evening." Suzie was still talking. "I live in that tiny house," she said, pointing across the piazza to the church. The house was a sort of lean-to attached to the mosaic-adorned gold cathedral. I mentioned this proximity to God and Church, which brought a snort of derision out of Suzie. "Believe you me, I'm no Julian of Norwich who used her proximity to the Church to go into heavenly trances. I prefer to keep my swoons right down to earth." She laughed at her own joke and told me that she thought entertaining lovers so close to the church was sort of a metaphorical middle finger to illustrate just what she thought of that institution as well. I had no idea who Julian was but knew these statements were close to sacrilegious, which made me a wee bit uncomfortable—you can take the girl out of the Church but it's never easy to take the Church out of the girl. I kept my mouth shut and my discomfort to myself, since I was knee deep in my vicarious enjoyment of her story and didn't want it to end. I didn't even mind that I'd been standing for forty-five minutes or that my toes were numb, my hands shaky from too many coffees and my chest rattling from the enormous number of cigarettes I had smoked. Suzie was the most exotic person I'd talked to in months and she spoke English. Then, just like that, Suzie said, "Let's go." Her transformation from storyteller to take-charge-of-Annie woman was impressive.

I don't know if the coffee or the enthusiasm of my new friend had anything to do with it, but outside the day had finally started to clear enough that I could appreciate what the tour book had been gushing about. To my right, back where I had gotten off the bus, was the now green-blue Bay of Salerno crashing against the beach. I wanted to just stand there and smell and listen, but Suzie was on the move. With my reluctant back to the sea, I saw the terraces and rooftops of the houses perched piggly-wiggly up the hill behind the town. They were peeking through the last straggler clouds that seemed reluctant to leave. Maybe they saw that I was now relatively dry and didn't want to miss out on an opportunity to drench me again. It was all quite beautiful.

Suzie propelled me away from the piazza, around the corner and into a tiny restaurant that was tucked in a side street. The sign over the door said "*Trattoria Maria*", which I thought had a nice ring to it. There were seven tables and no customers. It was still too early for any respectable Italian to think about eating and there weren't gauche tourists around in January to want lunch at noon. A counter ran from front to back and separated the eating from the cooking, but allowed people on either side to chat back and forth. A chubby man in a white apron was back there doing something over a fire that made me hungry, no matter what time of the day it was. Suzie, as if from habit, became the flirtatious kitten she'd been when we had entered the café. The chef was amused. I wished I didn't look quite so bedraggled and that I spoke Italian so I could partake just a little in the ritual. But as soon as the thought entered my head, the pleasantries were over and Suzie was getting down to business. "She needs an apartment," she said, tilting her head towards me. Bruno, the chef, looked me over, shrugged his shoulders in an "I don't know" kind of way and then turned to the phone.

While we sipped the tiny glasses of red wine Bruno had poured for us, Suzie explained that Bruno and his wife had built an apartment on top of their house and, being that it was January, it was sure to be empty. I thought having a cook as a landlord would be great. I imagined coming in to pay my rent and being thanked with a plate of pasta and another glass of this glorious wine. Then the door opened, and in came a no-nonsense-looking woman in housecoat and slippers. I thought immediately of Frau Sofia in Dubrovnik and my dream of free food and wine evaporated right then and there. She gave Suzie that universal, feral look of a wife who didn't trust single women, especially ones who look like Suzie. Bruno tilted his head in my direction and she came over with one of those landlady smiles, took my hand and said, "Hello, I Maria. How are you?" I was pretty sure those were the only words she knew in English so I kept my reply to a simple, "I Ana. Good, thank you." Maria motioned for me to follow her. I turned to Suzie but she shook her head and said, "I'll wait here with your luggage. Go have a look and see what you think." As Maria ushered me out the door, I saw her give Bruno one of those over-the-shoulder warnings that screamed "Watch out or get your balls cut off." Having heard Suzie's story, I thought she probably had good reason.

I followed her around the corner to a narrow opening between tall, gray stone houses that looked like they'd been around since Julius Caesar was ruling this land. The sign on the side of the first house said "*Salita Vagliendola*," which sounded too light and airy for this narrow, claustrophobic alley of stairs that stretched straight up in front of me. I knew now why Suzie had chosen to stay put on flat ground. Maria motioned me forward. I didn't know then, but would soon find out that there were 106 steps winding up the hill from the restaurant to the house. (I wrote Mom about the stairs. In one letter I said there were 106 and then later I upped it to 160. It could have been a typo, or maybe the number mysteriously increased the more times I walked up and down them.) There were no options to get up that I could see—no roads for cars or mopeds or a funicular, which I thought would have been a good addition to a town built up a hill. I had no choice but to start climbing or lose sight of Maria forever. As I trudged up, always ten steps behind her, I noticed the doors of these old houses opened right onto the steps, which I thought wouldn't offer a whole lot of privacy, especially if you were trying to sneak out undetected. Later I would see the women out every morning cleaning the steps in front of their houses with soapy water and brooms. I climbed on.

At step sixty-one by my count, I knew I had to stop or end up crawling the rest of the way to the top, where I had seen Maria disappear within a house. Here, chiseled out of the corner of one of the houses, was a tiny shrine to the Virgin Mary. It had to be some kind of a sign. Why else would I have stopped on this particular step? I'm always looking for blessings. After christening this my very own private Shrine to the Virgin Mary of the Sixty-first Step, I said a silent prayer to her for stronger lungs and a good sense of direction. Amen. I climbed on. When I finally reached the house where Maria had disappeared I was on stair number 106. I sat on the last step, chest heaving from the climb and every cigarette I'd ever smoked, and waited. She probably had enough time to do a load of wash and cook polenta in the time it took me to climb. When she reappeared, Maria ignored my distress and motioned me inside, where there were two more flights of stairs up to the apartment. I would be either dead or in great shape by the time I left here.

Maria unlocked the door at the top of the stairs with a flourish befitting her Italian heritage. She waved me into a hallway with four doors opening onto it, each, I was sure, holding some kind of surprise for me. Like a good Italian knowing the importance of food, she started with the kitchen. The first thing I saw was a huge, black, four-burner stovetop that resembled the one I had seen in the restaurant. This one was sitting on sawhorses hooked up to a bottle of gas underneath. It looked rustic and dangerous. Maria gave me a quick lesson on how to flip the button on top of the tank and then light up the burners with a match. I knew I'd worry about blowing up myself and everything around me while heating water for coffee. There was also a tiny refrigerator tucked under the sawhorse—which would hold nothing more than a couple of eggs and a bottle of milk. On one wall was an old, deep tin sink that I knew was meant to do double duty as dishwasher/washing machine. I didn't care because above it was a window that looked straight down to the facade of the cathedral, dazzling in the sunlight. I could see Suzie's lean-to, the piazza and people moving about. I was charmed.

We moved on to the sitting room, which almost defied the word since there were only two straight-back chairs tucked into a perfect square of a table. Nothing else. Maria must have read the disappointment on my face because she came back with another wave of her hand and a *"Domani."* This was my first venture into a southern Mediterranean country so I didn't really know the implications of that little word for "tomorrow," but I suspected I'd find out later rather than sooner. Room Number Three was crowded by comparison. It had a single bed, an old armoire that I noticed was propped up on a block of wood, another of those chairs that were sitting at the table next door and a spectacular view from the window. The sea and the sky stretched out in front of me, nothing else. I could even hear the roar of the waves as they hit the hidden cliffs. As I leaned out, I felt like the girl in that Dali painting—the one where she is standing at the window but you can't really tell if she's outside in the sea or inside in the room. Who cared about furniture when you had this view? I never closed the window again, not even when there were storms and the power of the sea sent sprays of water up the hill and into my bedroom.

I could tell Maria was ready to seal the deal when I questioned, "*Baño?*" "Hmph," she answered. "Hmph?" I replied. I was sure "hmph" meant the same in any language of the world and it was not good. Reluctantly she opened the fourth door. Now, everyone has their own definition of a "furnished" apartment, but, and maybe this was my American prejudice showing here, I always thought it included plumbing. In this bathroom there were only pipes and wires sticking out of the wall. Maria caught my eye and and said, predictably, "*Domani?*" I was starting to catch on now. Maria was doing a pantomime, pointing to the front door and down the stairs. I finally realized that she was telling me I could use their bathroom while mine was being furnished. Memories of Saturday-only baths in Dubrovnik crept into my brain. But then I thought that it might hurry up the renovations if I started taking hour-long baths in their *baño*. I told Maria, "*Si, graze. Cuonto?*" I guessed that would get me the price of the place. She wrote down what the rent would be, which was helpful since I hadn't mastered numbers yet. I calculated it in dollars and figured the $94 a month was great, especially since I had paid $140 in Dubrovnik for my one room. Maria held out her hand for a down payment and I answered, having learned well "*Domani.*" Going back down the 106 steps was a lot easier than going up. I told Suzie about the unfinished bathroom and scarcity of furniture and the promise of *domani*. She laughed out loud and then said something to Bruno that had him throwing up his arms and backing away as we left the restaurant.

Suzie drove me and my suitcases along the highway and up a side road that met the top end of the stairs. I was going to ask her why she didn't do this earlier to save me walking the 106 steps, but then I thought she had probably wanted me to factor the climb into my decision to take the apartment. As I got out of the car, she tooted her horn and yelled back at me, "Shops open at five. *Ciao.*" Then she was gone. She probably had a date, and the thought of that made me suddenly lonely. I shrugged on my backpack, grabbed a suitcase in each hand and carried them down a mere twenty-five steps to what would be home for the next three months.

My Own Version of La Dolce Vita

I knew from my experience in Dubrovnik that the best way to start feeling at home was to unpack, find a place for books and a journal and then go out and find cigarettes, bread, wine and food (in that order). I waited in the bare apartment until I heard the five o'clock drone of the bells and then went tripping down the stairs like I belonged. Shopping in Amalfi was not a straightforward A&P kind of operation. It wasn't even as easy as the mini-supermarkets in Dubrovnik. I knew this as soon as the bell over the door jingled and I put a foot down on the creaking wooden floor of the shop. Except for a pile of laundry soap and sacks of dried beans, everything else I needed was kept tantalizingly behind the counter in wooden cabinets reaching from floor to ceiling with a ladder attached for easy movement between products. An apron-sporting, arms-akimbo woman waited behind the counter for my order. I smiled a "*Buongiorno*" to her and then realized that there was probably a different phrase for the afternoon. Too late. She nodded and waited. I would have enjoyed the intimacy of this kind of shopping if I had known the words for the things that I wanted. The list of conversational phrases in the back of my guidebook were limited to "Please shine my shoes," "I would like tickets to the opera," and "Where is the hotel?" The only useful phrase was "*Quanto costo?*" which didn't help much since I didn't know the words for numbers and wouldn't be able to understand the answer. I made a mental note to myself to buy a dictionary and always carry paper and pencil.

I pointed to the things I needed—olive oil, sugar, coffee, a can of tomatoes and pasta. With each flick of my hand, she would climb the ladder and pull it and herself from one end of the cabinet to the next. I was impressed. When I had finished, it took a shockingly large sum of money to pay for it, even though the thousands of lira I handed over only actually translated to about four dollars in American currency. I then toddled off to get what bread was left at the end of the day, some garlic, vegetables, fruit and finally a bottle of wine to celebrate my new digs. It didn't seem like so much when I was buying it but I had already forgotten about having to climb those

106 stone steps of the Salita Vagliendola and the twenty more to get to my apartment. It was a hard-learned lesson as I trudged stair-by-stair home with my six bags. I never made that mistake again.

On the days she didn't have a lunch date, Suzie starting stopping by in the afternoon when the whole town was closed for siesta. She always came bearing gifts. I think she rightfully suspected that my budget didn't allow for a lot of frills and didn't want to take a chance that I'd have nothing to offer her. She'd always have a bottle of wine and my favorite brand of cigarettes and then maybe a tin of white asparagus, potato chips or a carton of olives. Whatever she brought we'd carry up to my private terrace and strip down to bras and panties and sunbathe on the floor. It was glorious with nothing but sun above us, waves crashing on the cliffs below us and nosy neighbors to ignore behind the windows around us. While we seriously worked on our spring tans, she'd tell me of her latest escapades with the boys in Positano or even further afield in Sorrento. "I've given up on Amalfi boys. They're too immature, and anyway I can't do anything here without the whole bloody town knowing about it." I told her I'd be happy with just one boyfriend who liked me and wanted to have a romance even without the sex. Suzie said I was delusional. I was still too shy to tell her I'd only had one sexual boyfriend in my twenty-six years. There are some things a girl just didn't confess in the middle of a sexual revolution.

On rainy days, when the low-lying gray clouds would surround my apartment and block any view from its windows, making it a claustrophobic prison, I would escape down the slippery stone steps and head for Suzie's place. She was usually home, since she hated going out in the rain and most of her boyfriends worked at jobs that couldn't be done in the rain, so were expected to be home for the midday meal with Mama. Suzie decided we should use rainy days for her to teach me Italian cooking. For our first cooking lesson, Suzie introduced me to artichokes. My only experience with an artichoke prior to Suzie's lean-to was having lunch with John Tully, a particularly snotty history professor at Ohio State. Being always in lecture mode, he pointed at me across the table and said, "The only blessing to living in this epicurean wilderness known as Columbus, Ohio, is that you can always find cheap avocados and artichokes." I kept quiet, since I wasn't even sure what those were, but I did know that I and all my family, friends and fellow Columbusites had just been insulted.

Suzie didn't care whether I'd ever seen, smelled or eaten one before. I was to eat one now. She held each artichoke up and admired it like it was a jewel. "Here," she said as she handed me one. "Watch me." With quick fingers she peeled off the toughest outer leaves and nodded at me to do the same. As soon as I started, she shouted "No! Stop! You're stripping away the good with the bad." It seemed I had a lot to learn about what constituted "tough" in an artichoke. I decided to just watch her and take notes for future reference. She slipped a paring knife into the base and pulled out a fuzzy little core. "This is the choke. Always take care removing the choke." She held it out for me to take so I'd recognize it the next time. I knew this was serious and so noted it in my book. She then snipped off the pointed tops and quartered each artichoke and threw them in a pot. At this point, I wanted Suzie to give me precise measurements and cooking times; instead she said, "Oh, just chop up a ton of garlic and throw it in," which she did. "Add two big glugs of olive oil and a little water and let these little beauties steam until you can put your fork through them." It seemed too simple to be as good as they smelled, cooking in that little lean-to kitchen. When they were perfect, we sat around her kitchen table with red wine and bread and ate the artichokes right out of the pan. There really was nothing snobbish at all about an artichoke. Later lessons included greasy pan-fried sandwiches with milky mozzarella and garlic, which were perfect for suppers on Sunday nights when all you had was stale bread. Sometimes I would pretend I was a creative cook and add ham or tomatoes or whatever was in my tiny fridge. Suzie tried to teach me how to make a casserole that included potatoes and pasta, but that was just too complicated and weird for my taste.

In return for all her generosity to me, I decided one day to take Suzie to Bruno's for lunch. It was an extravagant gesture for me so I basked in her appreciation. As we sat on our side of the counter, we watched Bruno make spaghetti sauce. Unlike his American cousins, Bruno didn't cook his sauce for four hours and he used a skillet, not a four-quart pot. There was no oregano in it and not even one of those secret ingredients that American cooks always insist make their sauce better than anyone else's. His was just fresh tomatoes, garlic, olive oil and splashes of salt, and was finished in about four minutes. It was breathtakingly simple and delicious. After watching him, I decided that I, too, like everyone else in Amalfi (and anywhere in Italy for that matter), would center my world around food. I started joining in with the women in the shops as they talked about what they were cooking for lunch. As my Italian lexicon grew, so did my knowledge of cooking. The women approved of this sign of domesticity in me. One day in the bread store, the owner gave me this basic lesson of life à la Italiano: it doesn't matter what your house looks like (which was a good thing, since hers was practically slipping down the hill), but your "*cara*," how you dress and, most importantly, what food you put on your table, were the only essentials of a good life. Amen.

Tre donne americane

In late February, everything changed. Suzie appeared at my door and said she had gotten a call from her mother saying that there was a woman from her church moving to Amalfi. She sat on my bed, head down, and groaned, "My life here is over." I thought she was being a tad dramatic until I remembered her goal of sleeping with all those men before thirty. Any church-lady friend of a mother would certainly put a damper on that one. But there was nothing to be done now. The lady was arriving the next day. As she heaved herself up she said, "Come with me to Naples. Otherwise I might be tempted to drive that red Beetle right into the Bay of Salerno." Then, just in case I needed more enticement to get out of Amalfi for the day, she added, "We can stop at Pompeii and see the dirty pictures, since I might not get another chance at decadence." Suzie tended to exaggerate at times.

As nerve-rattling as my first ride along the Amalfi Coast had been on the bus in the rain, it was nothing compared to the terrifying, life-threatening journey I was in for with Suzie. A VW Beetle is not a Porsche; it is not designed to go at high speeds or to hold to curves while equally death-wishing drivers are either tailgating you or coming straight for the windscreen. I tried closing my eyes, but that just made me nauseous on top of the fear. To make it worse, Suzie talked incessantly, which would have at least kept my mind on something other than the road except she had been in Italy long enough that she couldn't make a point without adding proper hand gestures. I recalled John Steinbeck's story about his car trip to Positano with a gesturing Italian at the wheel. He wrote that all he and his wife could do in the backseat was clutch each other for dear life and weep hysterically. I vowed that coming back I'd sit in the backseat, even without someone to clutch, especially since the return trip to Amalfi would be on the sea side where only a flimsy stone wall would separate me, the passenger, from the drop down the cliff. As we sped along the coast I wished that I had stopped by my Shrine to the Virgin Mary of the Sixty-first Step and offered a few prayers and promises before we left.

In Pompeii Suzie and I stood with a small group of tourists, waiting for the skinny guard in the too-small gray uniform to open the doors over what was promised in the tour book to be one of the naughtier frescoes in Pompeii. Italians are nothing if not dramatic, and this guy milked the moment to the max. I could almost hear a drum roll when he finally took off the big round key ring clipped to his belt and put the key in the lock. Of course, the first key didn't work, and he turned around and winked at us before he tried the next key and finally opened the doors. And there it was: the biggest penis in art that I have ever seen before or since. It even elicited a perfect "Oh" from the lips of a secular sinner like Suzie. We only got a minute to peek at it before the guard purposefully closed and locked the doors, then held out his hand for tips. It was the highlight of our whirlwind one-hour tour of Pompeii.

We were twenty minutes late getting to the airport, but we had no problem finding Valerie Lorraine Smith, since we practically ran into her as she stood smack dab in front of the doors with her purse clutched to her chest in a Queen Elizabeth hold and six red suitcases sprawled on the floor in front of her. I began to worry about how this substantial woman, the luggage, Suzie and me were going to fit in the VW. Suzie ignored me and the bags, thrust a hand out to Valerie and gave a cheery "Hi, Mrs. Smith. Welcome to Italy." I was impressed. Then, just like she had with me when I arrived, she took charge, hailing a porter and suggesting that Valerie and her luggage go by taxi to Amalfi. My hopes of sitting in the backseat were dashed.

Valerie Lorraine Smith was a single lady who had spent the last twenty years working as a secretary to the administrator of a mental hospital in rural Connecticut. After her mother died ten years previously, Valerie sold the house and, in order to save money for her retirement, moved herself and her few belongings into the wing of the hospital set aside for staff. She had a small suite located far enough away from the residents that she didn't hear their screams or smell the disinfectant. Valerie was practical, if nothing else, and figured the small space meant less to clean. I didn't think any of those things would ever entice me enough to live in such a place. I still remember my mother's cousin, Shirley, who was a nurse and lived in a mental hospital in rural New Jersey. Her stories of the place conjured up pictures of a dark, cruel world not so dissimilar to Lowood School, which as we all know was almost the end of poor Jane Eyre. Every Sunday Valerie

Lorraine would drive to her old parish for Mass. Afterwards, she'd listen while Suzie's mom entertained the Ladies' Sodality with stories of Suzie's adventures in Amalfi, of how much she loved living by the sea and how it was warm all winter long. Valerie Lorraine listened silently and began making plans—in her efficient, personal-secretary way—that would help her escape from the mental hospital and into a whole new life in Amalfi.

After the walk from the airport to the taxi stand, we both knew that Val would never be able to live anywhere in Amalfi except the center of town. She might be able to take the few steps to Bruno's, but never up the winding stairs to the upper neighborhoods. So Suzie did what any mother would have hoped she would do: she relinquished her lean-to apartment next to the church. After a wishy-washy protest, Val agreed, and was truly charmed by the sacrifice and delighted that she would be so close to daily Mass. I knew she'd be writing Suzie's mom a glowing letter about the generosity of her daughter.

Suzie moved in with me for a few days until she was able to track down the elusive Russian count who owned a flat high up on a hill above town. I had never laid eyes on him but heard wonderfully outrageous rumors about his orgies and his monumental irreverence toward all things Catholic. I thought Suzie would be an appropriate tenant for him. But at the same time, I think she was sorry to leave the center of this universe, where she could just drop into Bruno's or the café and flirt to her, and the men of the town's, heart's content. But Suzie, being Suzie, wasn't going to dwell on that. After all, she had her Beetle and could buzz up and down that hill faster than she could walk to the sea from the lean-to. But the real advantage was that she knew she never had to worry about surprise drop-in visits from Valerie Lorraine Smith.

During the first month of Val being there, Suzie declared that it would be a good idea if each of us stopped by on a different day to see her so she wouldn't get too lonesome. I thought this was sweet of Suzie until she stopped by a week later to tell me she was leaving with her Positano lover for a two-week vacation in Sicily, leaving Val in my charge. My jealousy must have shown on my face because Suzie took my hand and said, "Thank you for doing this. I'll make it up to you when I get back, I promise." What could I say? You stay here, Suzie, and let me go to Sicily with the Positano lover? No, never. Instead, I remembered all the lessons of sacrifice and good works drilled into me during those twelve years of Catholic schooling, and looked on this as money in my spiritual bank.

Visiting Val wouldn't have been so bad if it weren't for the predictability of the conversation. Each visit was the same. It would start with Val reciting her litany of complaints about all things Italian, including the cold (which she had been promised did not exist here), the way the priest said Mass, the nosy neighbors, and, highest on her list, the absence of Kellogg's Corn Flakes and Folgers Instant Coffee. That was my cue to suggest she try my favorite brand, Nescafé, but she was not to be appeased. "It wouldn't be the same." Once food products had been exhausted, she would move into the recitation of her secretarial experiences at the mental hospital, where she kept things ship-shape for Mr. Henderson, her saintly boss. "He was the director, you know, very important." Unlike me, and just like Susie MacNamara, she looked at her role as private secretary as a higher calling, a behind-the-scenes self-sacrifice necessary to keep America strong. Val just assumed that I missed the job as much. I always wanted to shake things up on those visits by spouting my views on the subservient, low-status, humiliating aspects of being a secretary. I never did. It wasn't in our script.

The Beginnings of *Arrivederci*

Suzie got back just as the rain began, which made me selfishly delighted, even though she did bring me back a souvenir plate from Sicily. That rain would stick around for seventeen days straight, making it the talk of every café, bar and store in the town. So much water rushed down the Salita Vagliendola I thought an ark, or at least an oar, would have been useful. I started to make detailed lists of everything I could possibly want in town so I would only have to slip my way down and back up once a day. It got worse. One morning on my descent down the gray, dark stairs, I stepped on something that was bigger than the usual bumps. When I looked, I saw that it was a very dead, very big, very black rat. There are few things in the world that I am genuinely terrified of as much as I am of a rat—even a dead one. I inched my way around it and headed to the Shrine of the Virgin Mary of the Sixty-first Step to ask for protection from other dead and alive rats, but she wasn't there. She had either been washed away by the deluge or taken in by a neighbor for safekeeping. Either way, I had to pray to an empty niche and hope that would do the trick.

The rain seemed to put a blue funk (as we used to say in the 1970s) over Valerie Lorraine Smith. She stopped complaining about not having her Kellogg's Corn Flakes and didn't even bring up Mr. Henderson in conversation. I suddenly missed him. She'd sit in her lean-to in the one comfy chair and just stare out without even seeing us as Suzie and I chatted about the rain and what we had had for supper the night before. Suzie didn't even get a rise from Val when she told us that she was really falling for her Positano boyfriend and ending her initial quest to sleep with as many men as she could before thirty. Something was wrong. Suzie held Valerie's hand one day and asked in a quiet, caring voice, "What's wrong, Val? Something's wrong, so please tell me." "I hurt," was all she replied. This put Suzie into action and out the door to get the doctor. He declared it arthritis, which somehow relieved Val who, even though she was still in so much pain she couldn't climb the steps going into the cathedral for Mass, at least knew why. "Well, my mother suffered her whole life with arthritis; a few weeks here and there won't kill me."

Since Valerie was feeling better, Suzie decided that it was time for the two of us to have a day away. She arrived at my door and said, "I'm taking you to lunch. Get dressed up!" This didn't take long since I only had one dress that I could still fit into and that made me look moderately sophisticated. We went to Positano to the Hotel Saraceno, where Suzie's boyfriend was manager. When I saw him look at Suzie, I knew she had found the romance that I had always longed for. Sigh. This hotel was a setting worthy of any love affair. It was built on top of and down a cliff overlooking the sea, with palm trees and gardens and Persian carpets, urns full of fresh flowers and mosaic tiles just like in Pompeii. I felt a tad embarrassed, a little Ohio girl in her not-so-sophisticated-after-all dress. Positano-boyfriend must have sensed this because he linked one arm in mine and another in Suzie's and walked us proudly and graciously into the dining room. When he'd gone to get our drinks, Suzie told me, as if this would make me feel better, "This is where Sophia Loren and Jacqueline Kennedy Onassis stay when they're on the Coast." I wrote my mom when I got home, *Mamma mia*, how the rich do live."

Valerie got worse and started to complain, quietly, about her pain. Suzie got a different doctor and this one ordered her to the hospital in Naples for tests. He would get the ambulance to take her there the next day. The speed of it all scared me. Suzie and I drove behind the ambulance. She didn't say much, and even I was too preoccupied to think much about dying from a head-on collision at high speeds on blind curves. After she checked in, we got Valerie into her flannel nightgown with tiny rosebuds on it and settled her down with the magazines and chocolates we had snuck into the hospital room. The doctors told Suzie to come back in a couple of days when all the tests had been run and they'd have something to tell us. Valerie looked like she already knew what they were going to say but would go along with the story, just to be true to her role as it was being written.

On the way home the sun came out, just as though it had not abandoned us for those seventeen long days. When we pulled into Amalfi it looked like the entire town was waving a welcome to us from the roof terraces, which were filled with white sheets hanging to dry. I was told in Amalfi that if you want really white sheets, hang them up in a full moon—no howling required. I figured that, after almost three weeks with no chance to hang sheets, even old folklore went out the window. Suzie and I went to Bruno's for something to eat and saw that all the prices on the menu were higher than they had been the day before. We joked about it being April 1, and maybe it was an Italian way to celebrate April Fools' Day.

Two days later, Suzie and I went back to Naples and found Valerie's room empty. The nurse told us she was in surgery, where it was discovered that it wasn't arthritis that she was full of, it was cancer. I can't remember the particular kind, but does it matter? The doctor told us she had, at most, six months to live. We could take her home at the end of the week. He suggested we call her family, but the only family she really had was Mr. Henderson, and I didn't think he would come. Valerie came back to Amalfi in an ambulance and we sat her back down in the overstuffed chair. Over the next few days I spent much of my time visiting her, telling her my own stories of home and old bosses and the good things I did remember after all about being a secretary. When Suzie came, Valerie asked her if she would please take her home to die. Suzie hid the sadness in her face from Valerie when she answered, "You bet." I knew that those two words came from a place of love somewhere deep down in Suzie.

Suzie spent her last week at the hotel in Positano to say goodbye to her romance and her Italian dream. She sold the red Beetle to Bruno for more money than it was worth, just to get back at him for raising his prices on us. Suzie didn't even look back when she climbed into the ambulance that would take the dying Valerie to the Naples airport and the flight back to New York. There, another ambulance would take them to Suzie's mother's house, where Valerie would die at least close to her mental hospital home. As I watched the ambulance head up the coast road towards Naples, I cried more for Suzie's loss than for Valerie.

As the sun got warmer and the air changed from winter cool to spring warm, Amalfi shed its winter coat and exposed its Official Tourists' Resort face. I was fascinated by the quick transformation. Overnight, everywhere—not just at Bruno's—prices increased on everything from cigarettes to my favorite brand of mozzarella. It wasn't such a big jump, and certainly not big enough to give up smoking, but it peeved me just the same. The little grocery with all the products behind the counter started giving me hard candy instead of coins for change. I told them I didn't really like that candy, but they insisted. I saved every piece and took it all back one day to use as payment for my can of tomatoes; they were not amused. Maria got in the spirit of the season by renting out two of the rooms in my apartment to an English woman and her kids. They were quite friendly and properly embarrassed by the situation, so much so that they treated me to a weekend of dinners out and cocktails in. But I knew there would be more tourists to follow, so I decided it was probably a good time to write to my old roommate's sister, Janine, who lived in France. My friend suspected that her sister was not being treated all that nicely by her husband's family and would I please go check it out.

While I waited for a reply, I spent my days hanging out at the beach, since there wasn't going to be one of those in the part of France where Janine lived. I got a letter from Suzie saying that Valerie Lorraine Smith had died peacefully and that Mr. Henderson hadn't even come to the funeral. What a rat he turned out to be. Suzie had gotten her old job back at Yale and didn't even mind the work, now that she had her own European adventures to brag about at departmental parties. I wonder if she included her Italian sexual conquests to really spice things up.

I was ready to leave when the letter finally came from Janine saying "Yes, please come." I bought a bus ticket to Naples, where I'd catch the train to France and from there, who knows. I said goodbye to the sea and the cliff and some of the neighbors on the Salita Vagliendola. Bruno invited me to lunch and raised a glass of wine to toast my goodbye. On my last trip down the 106 steps to catch the bus, I stopped at the Shrine to the Virgin Mary of the Sixty-first Step to say goodbye and to thank her for answering my prayers all these months, free of charge, even in the high season.

Cherry Pink
in Beaujolais Country

Villefranche-sur-Saône, France
May–September 1974

Not the Best First Impressions

There are approximately 270 cherries on a cherry tree and 80 cherries to a pound, give or take a pit or two. Thank the gods that I didn't know that little fact when I stood at the back door of Janine's house that June morning, facing the twenty-four trees in the back yard that I would be picking. I had made a contract with her mother-in-law, the imposing Madame Gravois. Truth be told, the woman scared me to death. I don't know why she intimidated me so much—she was a head shorter than I was, for heaven's sake! I think it was just her very proper demeanor and the fact that I didn't understand a word she spoke. When she said anything and looked in my direction, I was convinced that she was criticizing some gauche American mannerism of mine. I had good reason to believe this: the very first time I met her, I had committed the unforgivable social sin of arriving unexpected at her door, just as dinner was being placed on the table. If you ever want to get on the wrong side of traditional French people, interrupt their midday meal.

I had no idea such set protocols existed around mealtime anywhere in the world. I come from a family that cared little for such etiquette. If a stranger had shown up at my parents' door at suppertime to burglar the house, he would have been invited in for dinner and given the choice piece of meat.

The day I arrived at Madame Gravois's door, I had been traveling for twenty-four hours. It started with an early morning bus from Amalfi to Naples, and then an overbooked train from Naples to Marseilles, where I had to sit on the floor outside the lavatory while people walked over my head all night. I then traveled on the local buses until I arrived in Villefranche on the morning of the next day. Upon my arrival I was told I had just missed the bus for my last leg of this journey and there wouldn't be another one for two hours. I didn't have enough French francs to splurge on a taxi, so I walked. I showed the man in the ticket window the address Janine had given me and he pointed me out of town with three downward waves of his hand, which I took to mean I had a long way to go.

While I was still in Amalfi my friend Edith, who had been my last roommate in Washington, had written to me. I was surprised to get the letter, since we had not parted on the best of terms. You see, Edith had been trying for years to get a job in Europe. She didn't care what it was; she'd fill out applications for anything from nanny to farm worker to Peace Corps volunteer. I, on the other hand, had not done a thing except go to lunch with the right person one day, and by dessert I had myself a job for a year in Germany. Edith did not take it well. But here she was asking for my help, and the least I could do was to graciously offer my services. She wanted me to check up on her little sister Janine. It seems that Janine, who had gone to France for her junior year abroad to study the flute at the conservatory in Lyon, ended up learning more about the seduction of French men than music. She now lived in the countryside outside of Villefranche-sur-Saône with her husband, new baby, mother-in-law and, from the tone in Edith's letter, her two wicked sisters-in-law. Edith was convinced that Janine was locked in the basement, given porridge to eat and released only to clean the toilets and do dishes, and would I please stop by and check up on her.

Edith's letter arrived at the perfect time. All signs in Amalfi were telling to me it was time to move on. So I wrote to Janine and told her I'd be there, and could she please look for a place for me to live. I included my shopping list for "home": it had to (1) be very inexpensive—I mean ridiculously cheap but still clean and safe and all that; (2) come completely furnished with pots, pans, towels, sheets, plates, silverware and ashtrays (I would be smoking those lovely Gauloise cigarettes in the yellow pack); (3) be close to a bakery and market and a little café for a morning café au lait; (4) have a window to look out onto the street (I don't like apartments where you can't see what is going on outside. Okay, I will admit to a tad of *Rear Window* voyeurism); (5) come with landlords who speak at least a little English; and (6) include some earth to plant a garden. I always throw in this last item to my dream list of new places. It has never happened, but it stays on the list just the same.

I should mention right off the bat that there are two Villefranches in the south of France and this one is *not* the one that sits on the Riviera, home to the jetsetters with perfect bodies; this one is tucked in the middle of Beaujolais country and home to small business owners, farmers who come into town once a week to sell pigs, chickens and vegetables, and the good folks who buy them. And now me, on my way to the countryside to meet Janine.

The town ceased to exist after a few blocks. I was soon walking on a road lined with plowed fields and rolling hills topped with vineyards on both sides. There were no houses, no cars and no one to help me. I'm not sure anyone would have stopped anyway, since I looked like a bad caricature of the typical, overpacked American tourist. I struggled along with my two mismatched suitcases, my purse slung over my neck and a backpack that was so heavy it pulled me precariously off balance. (It was filled with unread books in English that Suzie had given me as a farewell gift and which I absolutely couldn't bear to leave behind in Amalfi, fearing I would not find others here.) In retrospect, the fact that no one else was on the road should have been my first hint that maybe everyone was otherwise occupied at this particular time of day.

Janine had given me a detailed description of the house and directions to get there from the bus stop. Unfortunately, she neglected to mention *which* bus stop. I guess she figured the house was distinctive enough that I would know when to get off the bus. I always find that when people give directions to places that are familiar to them they tend to leave out one very crucial item, like the address or the distance from town. Those kinds of small details would have gone a long way to relieving that pit-in-the-stomach fear I had of being left on this road at nightfall. But I was (and still am) a resourceful woman, so as I trudged along in what was becoming a muggish, too-warm-for-April late morning. I stopped at every bus stop along the way. Each time, I parked all my baggage and scouted the surroundings for what Janine described as "a big, white, ugly, square farmhouse on top of a hill with four windows and a door in front and a red roof. You can see it from the road."

I had walked and stopped about three hundred times when I finally saw the house (in actual fact, it was only three miles or so from town). There wasn't anything farm-ish or ugly about the place. I found it to be rather lovely in the way it sat regally overlooking its fields and vineyards. As I approached, I remained enchanted, until the door opened. A young woman about my age stood there with a question mark on her face that was bigger than the house. I pulled from my memory the few words I knew in French and said, in my best Ohio nasal, "Jay soois Ann, amee Janine." The young woman gave me and my bags a once-over. She had probably also detected the sweet odor of sweat and dirt that I carried around with me after traveling for what seemed like half of my life. Finally, she said, "*Un moment,*" and closed the door in my face.

There was nothing to do but wait, and so wait I did. When the tears were just about ready to roll down my face after having been left waiting for over ten minutes, Janine was there hugging me and bringing me inside. She seemed to be the same giddy, talking-a-mile-a-minute kid that I had last seen three years before when she came to visit Edith at our run-down, cheap, perfect apartment in Washington. I always felt like I had to accelerate my listening to keep up with her banter, but this time her waterfall of words came to a sudden end when I saw her eyes focus on someone behind me. That was when I met Madame Gravois.

She was wearing one of those sweater sets, this one pale blue, with the top button of the cardigan closed so the pearls hung perfectly. I hadn't seen anyone wear them much since the 1950s. I always loved the aesthetic of the look, the crisp well-put-together outfit where everything matched. I remember watching my older sisters getting ready for dates and putting on their salmon or aquamarine sets to pick up a particular hue in their tight straight skirts with kick pleats in the back. It's too bad that I never acquired their sense of style, nor had Madame, since there was not a hint of the same blue in her boxy tweed skirt. She said a polite "*Bonjour*" to me and shook my hand and then turned to Janine. I had no idea what they were saying, but I thought if I focused my eyes on her lips as she spoke maybe I would pick up a word here or there remembered from the brief but intense love affair I had had with French movies. But alas, it was not to be. What I did hear loud and clear was the message her body was giving to Janine, and that was not pleasant. Janine reacted by slumping so far forward I thought she was going to topple over at Madame's feet. Before that happened, though, Madame turned around abruptly and left us standing there in the foyer.

I started to say something, but Janine shook her head and put her finger to her lips to silence me. She motioned to my bags and we picked them up and climbed two flights of stairs to the tiny apartment under one of the eaves of the house, where she lived with Gisselle and Jean Phillipe. Once inside, that spunky young woman I remembered was resurrected, and the rant began against the French and living in the country and not in New York and being married to the selfish, spoiled baby boy of this family and having a mother-in-law like Madame! She stopped abruptly and said, "Oh, we have to go down right this minute because lunch is ready." I begged to at least wash my face, remove one layer of dirt from under my fingernails and comb my hair. She gave me two minutes for all three! I went into the *toilette*, but I should have avoided the mirror; twenty-four hours of bus and train and road scum had settled in my hair and around the creases in my eyes. What a first impression I had made. I was just too embarrassed to face them. Instead, I wanted to stay here with a paper bag over my head and never look at the family Gravois again. Janine was pounding on the door in a panic, saying, "Come on, we've got to go NOW. Time's up. *Allons-y*." She always mixed the two languages when she talked to me.

Lunch Is Now Being Served

They were all there sitting around the kitchen table when we walked in. Madame, at the head, gave a signal for Janine to introduce me to the family. She started with Jean Phillipe, the only male at the table, evidently the spoiled guy she had married. He charmingly stood up and took my hand and said, in English, "Any friend of Janine's is most welcome in our home." His two sisters, Claudia and Helene, stayed seated and nodded in my general direction. Then Janine picked up a perfect, tiny baby girl and introduced me to Gisselle, who giggled wonderfully upon seeing her mother. There was a harumph from the end of the table, and Janine put Gisselle down and took her chair. The main event was about to begin.

I had never eaten a genuine French meal in an authentic French house with real French people. I was nervous. This afternoon would be the ultimate test of what I considered my excellent skills in "Surviving Difficult Situations through Observation." I had started honing this skill when I was eighteen and working my first job at Ohio State University in the history department. For some reason I could never figure out (I had a pretty low opinion of myself in those days), I was always being asked out on dates by older men who were twenty-four and twenty-five. I had never dated anyone before these outings with the big boys, so I had a lot to learn. My older sisters were invaluable, offering me makeup tips, great clothes to wear and lectures on the rules about what you could and could never, ever do with a boy. I was impressed by their expertise. But once out of the house I was on my own. I figured if I just watched and did what the others did I'd be okey dokey. One night I had a date with a very sophisticated instructor in the department. I had checked out his CV when he asked me out and knew he had gone to Harvard and then Columbia and some foreign place I had never heard of. I knew the night was not going to go well when he got into the car after picking me up and said, "Your father is so bourgeois." I hadn't a clue what he meant but thought it sounded like an insult. We were going to go out with his sister, who was in from New York. We were meeting in her hotel room (going to hotel/motel rooms was high on my sisters' lists of absolute no's). The introductions were a bit awkward, since I really didn't know about shaking hands and I certainly wasn't going to hug this woman, so I just said "Hi." Then someone said, "What about a drink?" His sister asked for a Scotch on the rocks, and I said, following my survival rules for the night, "Same for me, thanks." They all watched as I took my first sip, waiting for me to gag or spit it out or something else to expose my naiveté. But they didn't get it from me; I was a girl in training, so I just pretended that my throat wasn't on fire and my entire esophagus destroyed for life. I just sat there and listened to them arguing some great issue I cared and knew nothing about, sipping the drink slowly as the ice melted, making it easier for me to finish the whole thing. It was a good first trial for my lifetime learning experience.

With this group around the lunch table, I knew I'd have to be particularly diligent about looking for subtle clues to the hows, whens and wherefores of eating a French meal. Madame orchestrated the entire event, starting with ladling perfect amounts of clear broth into lovely white bowls that were passed around the table silently until everyone had one. Meanwhile, Jean Phillipe filled wine glasses with a rich red wine that I prayed wouldn't put me to sleep right here at the table. I watched and waited, and when the others started to eat, I followed what they were doing. Conversation began almost as soon as the first spoon hit the soup. Since they all seemed to have forgotten that I was even there, I spent my soup time observing and trying to catch a few words that I understood. Janine was busy with Gisselle until Madame gave the signal for the next course. Janine cleared the soup bowls and brought out a stack of clean plates and then a platter with roasted chicken, potatoes and green beans, which she placed in front of Madame for serving. When we'd eaten that, Janine brought over a green salad. Maybe Edith was right about her Cinderella status within this family. I decided to get up at one point to help her, but I noticed that no one else at the table was even considering it; then I caught Madame's eye and knew that it might be a better idea if I just stayed put. The meal passed scrumptiously without any faux pas on my part, or at least I thought so.

Then the cheese platter came around, that final tribute to a good French meal. For some reason, Madame decided it should start with me. In all my training up to this point I had never encountered the protocol around the cheese platter. I was a Velveeta girl when I arrived in Europe, and then one day I had a found a fine substitute in *La vache qui rit*, which, even though not quite the yellowy melting goodness of my Velveeta, had satisfied my taste for the smooth blandness of manufactured cheese. Now, if that friendly, laughing cow had been on the platter, I'd have known what to do. I'd have just taken that little wedge, pulled the string and smeared it on my bread. There was none, of course. These were serious cheeses on this plate and I had no idea what they were or, more importantly, if I'd like them. What would I do if I hated the piece I took? Could I hide it in my napkin without anyone seeing? (I used to do that with the big chunks of cheddar that Mrs. Finnigan used when she made her macaroni and cheese for us poor, unsuspecting second graders at St. James the Less School. That cheddar never melted on the macaroni like the Velveeta my mother used so I wouldn't eat it, ever.) Also, I didn't know how many pieces of cheese I could take off this platter. What did I know? There could have been rules about such things, like there were in my house when I was a kid about the number of strips of bacon (three) you were allowed on Sunday morning. None of these questions left my lips nor showed on my well-trained face. The others watched and waited. It was a test. I decided that the best strategy would be to take a tiny piece of two kinds and pass the platter on. Then Jean Phillipe said, "Is that all? Try the Brie. I'm sure you'll like it." Which one was the Brie? At that point Janine must have decided that they'd had enough fun at the expense of her friend and said, "Let me cut you some." After I tasted that Brie I knew I was off Velveeta for life.

After coffee, everyone left the kitchen except for Janine, Gisselle and me. With no one else around to see, I washed dishes and swept the floor while Janine fed the baby. She told me she'd found me an apartment in town, but it wouldn't be ready for a couple of days, since the old tenants were particularly destructive and dirty, so it was taking longer to get it cleaned up. Madame had evidently, with some reluctance I'm sure, said I could stay here at the manor until it was ready. I wasn't really sure I wanted to take her up on her offer, but my shrinking funds and the thought of more cheese swayed me. Anyway, if I could get through that lunch I could get through supper and breakfast and whatever else came my way.

A Plan Is Hatched

The next morning Janine, with flute in hand, asked if I'd watch Gisselle while she and Jean Phillipe practiced a duet for an upcoming concert. I took Gisselle and a book and went outside and sat under one of the trees and looked out over the fields and vineyards. It was heaven for me. Here I was in Beaujolais country, home to famous wines I had never tasted until lunch yesterday. More importantly, I wasn't moving, or carrying hundreds of pounds of stuff, or worrying about timetables. I could just sit here and watch Gisselle sleep and think about what I would plant if I had a little patch of this earth.

I come from a family of gardeners. All my mother's sisters and brothers had gardens. When we visited them in the summer, the adults would head out back and not to the house. They'd talk about bugs and corn yields and the sweetness of this year's tomatoes. I think I must have planted a hundred gardens in my mind and not a one in the earth, but I always wanted to try. It didn't look like anyone was trying very hard here at the manor; things had that neglected sort of look about them. When Janine came to get Gisselle, I asked her why. She said she tried last year to have a little garden, but then Gisselle came and she had no time. Jean Phillipe and his sisters absolutely refused to do anything outside. "*Nous ne sommes pas les agriculteurs, maman,*" she said, mimicking their disdain for even the mere thought of working in a garden. Madame, on the other hand, loved this land. She had grown up here and always had gardens full of vegetables and flowers, but when her husband died suddenly, she had to start working in Lyon and had no time to give to the earth—not even to picking her cherries.

That's when the idea came to me of a brilliant way to ingratiate myself to this woman, to fulfill my dream of actually having my own little garden, to get my fill of country life while living in town and maybe even to score more lunches. I told Janine to tell Madame that I would volunteer to pick the cherries in June in exchange for a little plot of this land that I could use to plant my own garden. Janine burst into laughter. I really didn't think my suggestion was all that funny. She asked me, "Have you ever picked cherries?" Well, not professionally, but I used to steal them from the Eblins' tree next door. They were those sweet little red cherries like the ones embroidered on the border of my favorite dress when I was six. I'd wait and wait, and when I thought they were perfectly ripe, I'd go through the hole behind the lilac bush and climb the tree. More often than not the birds had already been there and taken a bite out of each cherry, but it didn't ruin my adventure. I don't know if that would qualify me as an experienced cherry picker here in Beaujolais country, but it would have to do.

That day at lunch Janine presented my proposal to Madame. There was some snickering from the siblings and an unreadable look on Madame's face. I thought that either she was totally shocked that anyone under thirty would offer to do anything when they weren't getting paid for it or she was seriously contemplating my offer. When she spoke she said just one word: "*D'accord.*" She sounded just like God. Janine was shocked and said in that squeaky voice she sometimes gets when she's nervous, "*D'accord?*" "*D'accord.*"

After lunch Madame marched us out to the yard and pointed to a small, weed-infested plot of land that had probably not been used in this century and said that could be my garden. We then headed off to a vine- and bush-covered shed, where she showed me a pile of long-abandoned, rusted tools that I could use. I was having second thoughts; you see, in my dreams, my gardens were always already in bloom, vegetables ripe on the vines, with birds chirping their happiness at my abundance. I hadn't really thought about the work involved in getting to the dream state. Was it too late to withdraw my proposal? Would I lose face forever and never get back to the lunch table? But there was no time to contemplate this because we were now on our way to the cherry trees. These were not Eblin-sized cherry trees; these were huge trees, with lots of thorny-looking plants at their base that I knew were designed to tear the flesh of gullible young American women who wandered into them. Madame told Janine to tell me that the cherries would be ready to pick in early June; she'd throw in an old bike they had there so I could get from town to the trees more expeditiously. I told Janine I had only ridden a bike once in my life and that was when Johnny Welsh tried to teach me in the parking lot of the Dairy Queen when we were twelve. I think he was really trying to teach me something else, but I didn't go there with Janine. She said, exasperated, "Oh, Ann, just take the bike and be happy you don't have to walk on top of everything else after getting yourself into this mess!"

Moving into Town

The next day Janine and I loaded the car with my suitcases, backpack, and old sheets and towels from the unused supply at the manor to drive into town to meet the Batalas, my new landlords. I walked the ancient, black, big-wheeled bike to the road and told Janine to go ahead of me. I didn't want her trailing. I was already nervous enough without having someone following me. Once she was out of sight, I started my wobbly way back along those three miles I'd walked, wishing at each rotation of the pedal that I was once again on my feet. She greeted me with an impatient sigh when I met her thirty minutes later at the edge of town. I walked the bike to my new apartment.

My apartment was in a neighborhood that didn't resemble any of my imaginings of what life in a quaint village in France would be like. There were no window boxes full of cascading flowers and charming old stone houses next to squares with striped-awning cafés filled with unattached men ready to buy me a drink. Here, on *Rue Général*, there was not even a shade tree, nothing to break the monotony of the grayness emanating from much-too-narrow sidewalks (could two people even pass one another on them?) and the fronts of the houses that looked naked for their lack of porches. To add the final nail to my coffin of jump-to-conclusions first impression of this place, there was a smoke-spewing factory at the end of the street. How could this be home? Janine ignored my groans and, remembering item number five on my list, handed me a French-English dictionary as we crossed the street to meet the landlords.

Landlords were a very essential part of my life in those days. They were sometimes the only people I knew, so if we didn't like each other at least a little bit in whatever put-together language we spoke, life could be pretty unbearable and lonely. But I knew immediately that I didn't have to worry about the Batalas. Janine had told me that Monsieur was originally from Yugoslavia and had left his farm there right after the war to come north to find work. He had found a job and later a French wife. Since I had lived in Yugoslavia I thought it would be a nice gesture if I said something to him in Croatian, just to get off on the right foot. As I shook his hand, I said the only words I remembered from Dubrovnik, "*Stretna Nova Godina.*" They both howled with laughter. That's when I remembered that it meant "Happy New Year" and not "Nice to meet you." I was properly and utterly embarrassed. But Madame Batala, or Madame B. as I started to think of her, who was considerably taller, wider and bubblier than her husband, came over and put an arm around me, thrust a bouquet of lily-of-the-valley into my hand and kissed me loudly on both cheeks, and then did the same to Janine. From that first meeting, I knew that it didn't really matter whether I understood what she was saying, or she me; we would get along just fine.

As she chattered on, she grabbed my arm and waved the others forward. She marched the four of us off the sidewalk and through a short passage that ended in a surprisingly charming, tiny courtyard, decorated with pots of geraniums and a small shade tree. Then Madame B. stopped purposefully, dug deep in her brown plastic purse, came out with a napkin and shouted, "*Minou, minou, minou!*" Janine mouthed the word "C-A-T." Out came a rather mangy, yellow, one-eyed cat who looked me over suspiciously, as if to say that he would be expecting the same treatment from me if I wanted safe passage through his turf. I tried to stare him down but got lost in the missing eye and knew I'd be adding cat food to my shopping list.

Madame B., keeping a jolly-sounding banter going, led us up the outside stairs to a landing with a choice of three doors, one next to the other. I remembered watching all those quiz shows on hot summer afternoons when I was a bored kid wanting to be somewhere else. I would yell at the contestants to "Pick the middle one! Pick the middle one!" convinced that it hid the beautiful bedroom suite. Monsieur took a single key out of his pocket and opened my middle door—no bedroom suite, but a tiny little foyer complete with umbrella stand and carved wooden pegs for coats and, unbelievably, two more doors, making a total of five doors, five keyholes and five doorknobs in a space so compact we couldn't all fit in it at the same time. I felt like I was in one of those British farces where illicit lovers slip out one door while an unexpected husband arrives through another.

I found out much later that the reason there were so many doors was that Madame B.'s first husband (now deceased), who had done all the work on this apartment, was absolutely phenomenal at salvaging bits and pieces from buildings that were being torn down. He seemed to have a particularly special talent for spotting doors, and since he didn't have any place to store them and couldn't bear to put them back on the rubbish heap, he just put them all here as a sort of majestic entrance to his masterpiece.

But once inside the apartment there was not another door to be seen, not even around the toilet and sink that sat rather brazenly exposed in a corner of the huge kitchen. Sadly, I noted that there wasn't a tub or shower, either, with or without a door. Madame B. caught me staring and said not to worry, she'd bring a curtain by the next day, but she didn't say anything about a tub.

I couldn't stay disappointed long because Madame B. was so magnificent to watch as she gave me the tour of the apartment. As she went from stove to refrigerator, plates to pots, covering all the essentials on my list, she reminded me of watching Betty Furness in the 1950s, opening the doors of refrigerators and saying, "You can be sure if it's Westinghouse." I hoped all my *bons* and *très jolies* here and there were enough to show her my appreciation. But just as she was about to show me the kitchen sink and its hot water tap, I gave a pleading eye to Janine that begged her to please tell Monsieur and Madame that, yes, I'd love to live in this apartment of five doors and could we sit down and drink on it. And that's when Monsieur Batala vanished.

One minute he was sitting at the kitchen table and the next he was gone. Now before you even go there, yes, I know this was the 1970s, but I was not on any hallucinatory drugs or having flashbacks. He just was like poof, gone. Mind you, he was a pretty small guy and hadn't said boo since Madame had started her show. He had just sat at the table watching her with a sweet smile on his face, as though he were surprised and delighted that she belonged with him. But I don't care how quiet and tiny he was, I would have noticed if he'd walked by me to the kitchen door. Where was he? Madame and Janine did not seem concerned in the least bit—maybe one or the other of them was indeed expecting a lover to slip in from one of those five doors. Then I saw Monsieur coming out of the wall in the next room; literally coming out of the wall. Now this was something that I could say *Oui!* and *Oui!* again to. Monsieur had come through a secret passage that led to a tiny hallway and into my bedroom, now how cool was that? Mind you, it was not quite as fancy as the escape hatch I had seen at Versailles, through which Marie Antoinette snuck out while the cake-eating mob descended. But it would do. I could imagine already my French lover slipping through it while I lounged in something see-through in the boudoir beyond. Alas, it never happened, but a girl could dream. So this would now be home. It had enough quirkiness to satisfy my adventuresome side and enough locks, hot water and cleanliness to calm my homebody side. I would be content for a while.

A Saint and a Kilo of Sausages

The Batalas were regular visitors. They adopted me just like they had Minou, who I think was more than a little jealous. Not having children of their own, they picked up waifs like us to spoil, so we would be a little less alone in the world, for a while anyway. Every Wednesday they would show up with scraps for Minou and bags full of food from their farm for me. There was a ritual to those Wednesdays; when I heard Madame crying "*Minou, Minou, Minou,*" I'd go out the wall of three doors and down the stairs with my friendly "*Bonjour*" at the ready. Monsieur would always shout "*Stretna Nova Godina*" when he saw me, liking that we had our own private little joke going on. Then he'd carry all the bags upstairs and sit and watch as we women unloaded them and I oohed and ahhed and said *merci* hundreds and hundreds of times. I ate well on their generosity and good farming. Early in the summer there was sweet lettuce and radishes, and then later leeks, courgettes, Swiss chard, onions and carrots and always, always flowers—lily-of-the-valley, then roses and zinnias. Madame B. would arrange them in the one vase in this apartment of doors, and when she set the finished product in the center of the table I knew it was time for me to make coffee and bring out some cake or cherry pie or cookies. And there we would sit, the three of us who'd come to this table from different places and different languages but who could now sit and communicate and be friends for a little while.

Sometimes they would show up and announce that we (not Minou, who snorted his displeasure at being left out) were going on an excursion. We'd pile into their ancient *Deux Chevaux*, with Madame keeping up a constant commentary on everything we passed in time to the putt-putt of the engine. We'd head out to the countryside to gather herbs for tea that would cure my summer cold, or we'd go to the home of one of their friends who had particularly good water in their well. One day we went all the way to Ars for a celebration in honor of St. John Vianney, their own local miracle-performing saint. I had never come across this St. John when I used to page through the big, brown volume of the *Lives of the Saints* that my mother always kept within reach of little hands on the bookcase in the living room. I loved that book, especially the pictures of the saintly martyrs who had to endure eye gouging or hot pokers to the chest or some equally painful-looking torture, all to show their love of God. I always said a little prayer as I looked at them to ask God that if I was really good and went to First Friday Masses for a year would he please not ask me to show my love by having my fingernails torn out, Amen. This St. John must have prayed too, because he had earned his sainthood on good works and modesty, not bodily torture.

When we got to Ars the Batalas shuffled me into the church, where the still-intact body of the goodly saint was enthroned over the main altar with a white wax death mask over his face (just like the one I saw of Abraham Lincoln, but not the same face, obviously). I had always found the churchly practice of displaying mummified bodies, severed toes and ring fingers or locks of hair that appear to keep growing after death just a little too gory to stir holy thoughts in me. But before this sacrilegious thought could properly enter my head, the Batalas were up and headed for the door in the time it took to say one Our Father and one Hail Mary. We snaked our way through the crowds at the outdoor market that sold sweets and chips among the holy cards and other mementoes of St. John. They didn't ease up on their trot until we reached Monsieur Matel's *boucherie*. Unbeknownst to me, this was the home of the best, rarest white sausages this side of Lyon. Monsieur the *boucher* only made them a few times a year as his own special form of praise for the local boy-made-saint (and a way to make a lot of money on a holy day). The Batalas bought a kilo for themselves and told the *boucher* to wrap up two little ones for me too. I felt blessed indeed.

Making a Grand Entrance

As sweet as the excursions with the Batalas had been, I was anxious to start planting the seeds I had picked up at the market. But I hadn't heard a peep about the ripeness of the cherries for picking. I didn't think it would be right to start the work on my garden until *after* I had picked the cherries. You see, in my thinking, picking the cherries had to be done first in order for me then to have the right, even the privilege, to go out and sweat over the weeds and dried dirt of my own little garden. Actually, the real reason I didn't go was that after my first encounter with this family, I was more than a little nervous about just showing up there without an invitation. So while I waited for the ripe-cherry report, I contemplated how I could diplomatically go about having shower and washing machine privileges (I had neither in my apartment) incorporated into my contract. Washing body and underwear had become obsessive agonies to my existence. Then one day Janine stopped by to inform me that the cherries were ready and Madame expected me at the manor the next morning to begin the cherry picking (no prior notice here, just a BE THERE OR ELSE order). I took advantage of the moment and presented her with my proposed amendments to my contract with Madame. She looked doubtful and said I could try if I wanted to, but not to get my hopes up. Thankfully, she did tell me to go ahead and bring my laundry and my dirty body the next day and, if nothing else, she would sneak me into her bathroom for a shower.

That afternoon I went to the hardware store and bought one of those one-piece jumpsuits like painters and garage mechanics wear (mine did not have a little oval with "Ann" scripted on it). Having seen those trees, I wanted to be sure that my arms and legs were protected from harm. Then I got a cardboard box from the market and found a rope under the porch of my apartment. The next day I fixed the cardboard box on the back of the bike and loaded into it my laundry, shampoo and soap (I didn't want to presume I could use theirs) and a can of sardines and crackers (in case

I wasn't invited for lunch), and then headed out of town for my first day on the job. I thought it was wise to get off the main road with my uneven load and still-underdeveloped riding skills and take the back road that I had discovered on one of my explorations around the town. The ride was not as smooth, since it was full of gravel and dirt and potholed from winter rains, but I didn't have to contend with automobiles and more experienced French cyclists. Anyway, I was a woman on her way to work in the fields, and being rattled from head to toe just seemed more appropriate for this farm worker.

I was doing really well, when things went a bit awry, and my first day almost ended before it even began. When I reached the final hill to the manor I saw Janine in the yard waving to me and, like a seasoned rider, I reached a hand up confidently to return the greeting. Not a good idea: the front wheel slipped on the gravel, causing the bike to start to fall while throwing me into a perfect spin over the handlebars. I landed on my hands and knees and started a slow slide the rest of the way down the hill. When I came to a stop I realized the whole family had watched my descent. I crawled around, too embarrassed to stand up and face them, especially as I was picking up my contraband dirty underwear, towels and shirts that I wanted to secretly wash in their washing machine from the road. I could hear them clucking as they picked up the bike and the laundry and got me on my feet again. I hate being fussed over, especially when I have done something very embarrassing that inadvertently brings me attention. I'd rather just crawl away somewhere private and lick my wounds, except I couldn't see my wounds until they were reflected on their shocked faces. It didn't look good. Jean Phillipe took the bike and the cardboard box and walked them up the hill while Janine and Claudia each took one of my elbows and shuffled me along as though I was seventy-two. Madame was waiting in the kitchen with a basin of warm water and iodine to swab and sting me back into shape. She had taken the day off work to give me my first lesson on Picking French Cherries, so there was no way I was going to let a few bruises and cuts (well, actually, they were everywhere) keep me from the job. I told Janine to tell her I would be back in a minute to start picking. Janine just shook her head at me and relayed the message to Madame.

My stubborn pride has often gotten me into stupid predicaments, but when I went into the bathroom to get suited up and saw the black eye, scraped knees and a big knot getting larger by the second on the top of my left hand, I thought this may make my top ten list of all-time stupidities. (Months later, when the bump on the back of my hand had gotten even bigger and I was in my phase of worrying about the seven signs of cancer, I asked a medical student in Seville if he thought it was a cancerous growth. He didn't bother to answer.) But no backing out now: Madame was waiting in the orchard, along with the twenty-four trees. As I pulled on the brand-spanking-new one-piece I cursed myself that I hadn't washed it first, so it would have softened up a bit, but that would've been impossible since I was here to do the wash! The stiff material rubbed painfully against each and every scratch and scrape on my body, even finding some new ones I didn't know I had. I wondered if I could save up all this pain in some kind of penance bank for some future transgression against all things holy. Bruised and suited up, I went to meet Madame and the cherries.

It seemed that Madame accepted it as natural that I would be here, even though she had witnessed my fall firsthand. I think I moved up an inch in her estimation when she saw me heading towards her. She handed me a small green bucket, about the size of one a kid might take to the beach, and motioned for me to follow her to the first tree. Since Janine was busy with music and taking care of Gisselle, I was on my own for the first time with Madame. This teaching experience was going to be show-and-tell all the way.

Picking French Cherries

When you are right under a cherry tree, it's hard to see the fruit for the forest of leaves. Madame had the eagle eye of an expert, and she plucked those cherries so fast her first pail was filled and she was started on the second one before I had even tossed a few fruits into my own. It was because, she had stressed emphatically, using multiple hand gestures that I perceived as threats, no cherry should leave the tree without its stem intact. This slowed me down considerably, since it takes a certain *je ne sais quoi* to twist that cherry just right so that the cherry and the stem come off the tree at the same time. I ate a lot of cherries that first morning trying to hide my mistakes from Madame's eye. But just when I was giving up all hope and despairing once again about my decision to take this on, I got it right. My wrist action and the cherries started performing in perfect harmony; it was beautiful.

Madame and I worked the rest of that morning in a kind of silent camaraderie. Before the first tree was finished, we had developed an easy rhythm to the work; we would take turns emptying the full pails in the crates at the edge of the orchard and bringing back more empty ones. I felt like I was gaining her respect, or at least I perceived it as that. Maybe it was just working her land once again and not sitting in an office in Lyon that made her seem less formidable. By the time Janine came down to get us for lunch, we had finished one and a half trees. Madame announced just then that she would be going back to her office in the afternoon, so I'd be handling the trees on my own for the rest of the day.

When I stood up after lunch, every ache in my body was magnified to the same degree as the number of cherries I had picked. I was not in good shape. Janine suggested that I regain my sanity and give up. Every cut, scratch and bruise from my morning fall agreed with her and began to protest any movement toward the orchard. But I couldn't give up now—I had made a deal. How could I ever come back here again if I didn't do what I said I would? And, anyway, there was still my garden to get from dream stage to reality. Janine clearly thought I was crazy and said so as she rubbed my shoulders and patted my head. As a consolation, she said she'd do my laundry, since all the family would be gone in a few minutes and no one would know the difference. So, with honorable resolve, I returned to the trees.

By the end of the afternoon I had finished the other half of the tree from the morning plus one more, which left twenty-one trees to pick. The fruit would be rotting on the branches by the time I got to the last one. I felt like Sisyphus rolling that stone up that hill over and over again; I would fill my little green pail, empty it and fill it again, but never seemed to get close to the finish line. When Madame came home from work and saw me still in the orchard, she called out something to me, but I just waved, thinking she was saying, "Keep going, girl, you have twenty-one more trees to go!" Janine was there and shouted out the translation: "Stop working and get up here right now, you fool!" I'm sure it was a loose translation.

I shouted back that I had to finish this last pail, which was half full. Much earlier in the day, through a series of charades which involved holding up fingers and creating an imaginary scale, Madame had explained that the reason we used these little green pails was because each one held half a kilo, and this way we would know how many kilos we had picked at the end of the day. So there was no way I could dump a half-full one into the crate at the front of the orchard. I am a Capricorn through and through, which can be boring, I know, but reliable always. I filled up the rest of the pail, then limped my way up the hill to where Janine stood with Madame. In rapid French, Madame issued a series of what sounded like orders to Janine, who in turn gave them to me: It is too late for you to ride the bike home tonight. You are to go inside and have a long soak in the shower (Janine interjected, "Your clothes are clean, so you have something to put on"). You are to have dinner here tonight and stay over. You have picked all the cherries that I need for my use but you can pick as many cherries as you want for your own use. With the translation ended, Madame turned and walked back into the manor. I believed she had just given me her stamp of approval for my first day on the job.

A couple of days later I was back in the orchard. This time I rode the bicycle on the paved road, taking my chances with automobiles rather than gravel. I had left my one-piece at the manor and Janine had washed it for me, and when I put it back on it was softer and marked with well-earned cherry stains. I wore it with pride as I marched from the house down to the trees to start my second day as a cherry picker. I was never one to turn down free food, in whatever form it was offered, and knew that was a big reason for my doing this. But there was something else driving me back to the orchard. It was an indescribable sadness somewhere deep in my soul that I felt when I thought about all these cherries that would rot out here on the trees and never be enjoyed or thanked for being so delicious. I would never confess that feeling to Janine nor Madame. I knew they would think I was being melodramatic or just plain stupid.

I picked like a woman driven—not worrying quite so much if the stems were there or not. These were my cherries and no one would know the difference. At the end of my second day I had cleared a total of six trees and knew I really couldn't use any more cherries in the three months I had to be here. It seemed like such a waste, but I asked forgiveness of the unpicked trees. As it was, I ended up with kilos and kilos of the delectable fruit. I couldn't give them away because the only people I knew in Villefranche were my landlords, who had trees of their own, and of course Janine, who would have thought me totally over the edge if I had offered any to her. The only thing to do was to carry my bounty on the bike to my apartment and start thinking of creative ways to use them.

Life Is Truly Just a Bowl of Cherries

I made jars and jars of preserves from a recipe Janine had translated for me from Madame's cookbook. Since I didn't own a measuring cup or spoon, I guessed at proportions and spent hours picking pits and stems out of the brew as they floated to the top of the bubbling sugary mess cooking over a low heat. The kitchen and I were specked with red splatters and I prayed that my sweet landlords, Madame and Monsieur Batala, would not choose this day to come for a visit.

In all, I knew I had enough jam to last me beyond my three-month stay here. I froze those I hadn't preserved, which meant I made everything with cherries that summer: I basted chickens with them and stuffed some inside for good measure; I cooked them as a glaze with pork chops; I chopped them in salads and pretended they were vegetables when I didn't have anything else around. My first attempt to make a cherry pie without having my mother a phone call away to give me instructions and lectures was a disaster, but I ate it anyway. And I spread preserves on my baguette every morning. Turns out, the more fermented the cherries became, the more alcoholic they were, so my morning baguette was often accompanied by a bit of an alcoholic buzz. Even though I ate those cherries with my three meals every day and as endless snacks, I never got tired of them, and I think that was because I had picked each and every one myself.

I still went to the manor a couple of days a week that summer to work on my little hopeless plot of land. I had such a lovely routine. I would leave the apartment in the early morning and buy my bread at the *boulangerie*, where the lady in the white apron would call out, in the same timbre as the ring of the bell over the door, "*Bonjour, madame.*" I'd say. "*Un baguette.*" Then I'd come home and fix myself a Nescafé and cut the still-warm bread into several thick slices and smear them with fresh butter and thick layers of cherry preserves. Then I'd pack up my laundry and a snack that closely resembled my breakfast, climb on the old black bike and head out to the country for the day to pretend I was farming. Nothing really grew in my garden except some scrawny Swiss chard and radishes. I didn't care. I was still happy with my efforts. Madame would come out some days and tsk and cluck at the vegetables. She told Janine that I should have checked the phase of the moon before I planted and now all was lost. But it wasn't all lost, because my little hopeless garden got me out of town and into the country twice a week; it gave me a chance to take a shower and do my laundry; and, of course, there was always lunch.

One day when I was out in my garden, Janine called me to lunch. There seemed to be a more festive air around the table; Claudia and Helene even smiled when I came in and, I think, asked me how the gardening was going. After lunch, no one ran off to music practice or back to work or off with friends like they usually did. Then Madame announced that "it" was ready to try. I didn't know what this meant but everyone else started clapping. I looked at Janine who gave me that "I'll tell you later" look. Madame took down a tall glass container from the shelf that was filled with cherries and liquid. She spooned some cherries into tiny clear-glass bowls and passed them around. I had never tasted cherries like these before, and began to feel slightly light headed as I ate them. While everyone oohed and ahhed to a proud Madame about the cherries and drank their coffee, Janine filled me in on this ritual. Evidently, Madame had inherited, along with the land, the right to make bootleg alcohol. She was only permitted by law to make a limited number of bottles each year. The recipe that was handed down through generations of her family was a secret that no one, not even her children, knew. For some ancient and mysterious reason, the recipe was not going to be passed on to Jean Phillipe or Claudia or Helene; when Madame died, so would the secret. So as Madame grew older, this ritual took on even more significance to the family.

When everyone had finished eating their cherries, Madame poured thimble-sized portions of the liquid from the jar into tiny crystal glasses. Once we all had a glass in hand, Madame raised hers in a toast, first to her ancestors and this land that had supported them all these years, and then to the twenty-four cherry trees whose sweet fruit were the essence of this treat. Then she turned to me and gave me a *Salut!* in thanks for picking the cherries that had allowed her to make this magic happen once again.

Saying Goodbye

By August it became apparent that I would never be a farmer. My poor little plot of vegetables was painfully stunted from lack of fertilizer and daily watering. There was nothing I could do about it. I knew I couldn't, and wouldn't, go out to the manor every day to water, and there wasn't anyone there who had the time or inclination to do it for me. After three months of my mooching all those incredible lunches, I started to feel a shift of the welcome mat. It was always properly and discreetly done, a word or sigh when I walked in the house, usually from Claudia or Helene—Madame was much too proper to do anything so obvious. But I knew just the same. Janine confirmed my gut feelings and suggested I come out after lunch on Thursdays to do my wash and have my shower when the rest of the family would be gone. I now knew what Adam and Eve must have felt like walking out of Eden.

Most days I didn't mind staying in town, especially if the market was going on and I could go down and pick up the vegetables I couldn't grow myself. I always loved the smell of the wet earth that still clung to the leeks and potatoes and the clucks of the chickens that they sold upstairs. Other days I'd ride my bike down to the river and pretend it was the sea and I was sitting on a beach. It never worked. Or I'd take my book and lunch out to the park and sit and watch what I was sure were illicit rendezvous as men and women drove into the parking lot in separate cars and left together in one. The Batalas still stopped by to visit, I think more for Minou than me. They knew I'd be going soon. Since I wasn't going to the manor as often, Janine started visiting me when she was in town. I think it gave her a chance to be the young girl she still was inside her motherhood. We'd laugh and talk about home and family and eat lots of cherries so I could empty the freezer before I left.

But that didn't take care of Sundays. When Sundays came along no one stopped by to visit; even Minou seemed to go into hiding. There seemed to be a universal rule declaring Sundays "Family Only" days, visitors not welcome. It always seemed that everyone except me had something to do. I knew that Janine would go to Mass with Jean Phillipe's family and then home to help prepare a large Sunday dinner at the manor. I was never invited—never on Sundays. I wondered if she set a plate for Jesus the way her and Edith's mother used to do. I doubted it; it was the kind of thing her inlaws would have frowned upon and used as another reason to shake their collective heads at this young American under their roof. The Batalas, childless as they were, used their Sundays to visit Madame B.'s relatives, who were scattered around the countryside. They told me they always ended the day with a visit to the cemetery to clean the weeds off the first Monsieur's grave. I thought it showed what a loving, sweet relationship these two had to include the memory of the other Monsieur into their Sunday ritual.

When I was young and at home and sad because it was Sunday, my sister Susie always used to tell me that I'd have to work on that situation, or else I'd be unhappy for one day out of seven for the rest of my life, and that was a lot of days. So that's why I decided that this Sunday, almost my last in Villefranche, I would take her advice and, instead of watching my neighbors taking their Sunday stroll, I'd leave my kitchen window and take my own walk through the neighborhood. The day was hot and overcast, making the air seem almost too heavy to breathe. It reminded me of the emptiness I felt when I read *The Stranger* for the first time and followed Meursault through that too-hot and too-bright Mediterranean day. I bet it was a Sunday. Maybe the memory was also stirred because of the neighbors I passed, who would have fit quite nicely into that particular Camus story. I have to say they looked different at street level. We'd smile or make silent eye contact; sometimes there was a tip of the head, but we never spoke or acknowledged that, as we shared this narrow sidewalk, we were a little less alone than we would have been in our rooms. I wondered if this was a ritual that all foreign workers followed for Sunday afternoons everywhere in the world, and if Monsieur Batala had walked the streets when he came up from Yugoslavia before he found love and companionship with Madame.

I walked a long time that day through the streets in my neighborhood. It was like saying goodbye. After a while I didn't pass any more of my neighbors and only had the quiet and stillness of the Sunday afternoon as my companion. Then I heard music that stopped me cold. It was coming out of an open window where a white lace curtain was blowing gently, as if it were accompanying the song. Leonard Cohen was singing "Hey, That's No Way to Say Goodbye." Suddenly I was back in that apartment I had shared with Edith, sitting on the dining room floor and clutching that Virgin-in-Flames album cover while I cried over my first broken heart. The album had arrived in the mail with a letter telling me that the man into whom I had tucked my heart for the past two years had met someone on a trip to Nassau and married her that past weekend. Maybe he thought this poetic gesture would leave him in a positive space in my heart forever. I smiled. Here on the streets of Villefranche, the song just made me feel less alone and, oddly, a bit happier. I stood outside that window and listened to the whole album. If anyone had come by and asked me why I was standing there, I would have told them that I was having a Sunday afternoon visit with an old friend.

INTERMEZZO
Two Stories from Seville

Seville, Spain
September 1974–April 1975

Garlic and Love in the Afternoon

My mother never taught her six daughters how to cook. Well, she didn't teach her six sons either, but they all, except one, ended up with wives who took care of filling their stomachs. I'm sure there was nothing sinister about leaving us girls challenged in the kitchen—she was probably just too tired from the effort to come up with meals for fourteen people every day, three times a day. Whatever the reason, I reached my twenties with a tiny repertoire of meals—macaroni and cheese made with Velvetta, green beans topped with mushroom soup and onion rings (all from cans), and fried dumplings—none of which I could translate into my food life in Europe. I had added Frau Sofia's *Grah* and Suzie's juicy mozzarella sandwiches to my repertoire, but I still wasn't prepared for what I would find in Seville in 1974. Food became an obsession, even more than in Italy. I spent all my time thinking about it, shopping for it, preparing it and cleaning up after it. This passion erupted when Martha arrived. Before Martha I cooked; after Martha I was a cook.

Martha arrived at my door about three months after I had moved to Seville. I didn't know who she was—she turned out to be an acquaintance of Pam, the artist woman who had lived in the flat before me. Every year Martha would show up at her door for a two-week stay. Unfortunately, Pam had not bothered to tell Martha neither that she had moved in with her current lover nor that I was now living in the flat. Martha was a straightforward, no-nonsense American with a very thick Brooklyn accent. She wasn't particularly embarrassed or uncomfortable about the situation; she just plopped herself down and said, "Now, what are we going to do about this mess?" I didn't feel that it was my mess at all, but somehow Martha made it our equal dilemma.

Martha was odd looking. It was as though none of the pieces of her face fit together, like a Picasso painting. She wore large thick-framed glasses and had frizzy hair. I also noticed that, for a woman in her late twenties, she had a lot of acne. Just as I began to think that she possessed no redeeming feature, I saw her mouth. She had the poutiest, sexiest full lips I had ever seen this side of Hollywood. (I'm particularly jealous of thick-lipped women, since mine were once described by an ex-lover as "hard to get a grip on.")

Martha explained that she came to Seville every year for two weeks to see an acne specialist, as it was much more affordable in Spain than in

New York. That's when she said, in her broadest Brooklynese, "The acne is so bad on my back that if you connected the dots it would be a perfect picture of the Statue of Liberty." Martha worked in a law firm in New York and saved up her vacation time and money to make this annual trip. She told me she had met Pam the artist during one of her visits and, using her "fellow American" ploy, talked her into renting the room at the back of the apartment.

I didn't have a telephone to call Pam. If I had wanted to check on Martha's credibility, I'd have had to walk down three flights of stairs, around the corner, and up two streets and post a note on her love-nest door. She'd have to do the same with a reply. The effort seemed somewhat rude with Martha right in front of me and would have been a very bad way to start our friendship. I decided to just trust Martha. Besides, I had nothing of value to steal and she didn't seem the type to have an ax hidden away in that suitcase. I also thought it would just be fun to have someone to hang out with at cafés and bars. But most of all, I invited her in because she made me laugh.

As she made her all-too-familiar way through my bedroom and into the back room, she called out in an "Oh, by the way" manner that she may have a friend over sometimes, since she was also visiting Seville to rendezvous with her very married Spanish lover. Well, she didn't use the phrase "very married"—I found that out a couple of days later when we were cooking together. The thought of married men getting it both ways always riled me. I felt it was just so unfair to both women involved (this could also have had a bit to do with the fact that my last boyfriend had turned out to have a wife at home…the rat). However, I kept my opinions to myself and vicariously enjoyed every story of her romance with Pedro.

Our lives took on a very easy pace; whoever was up and dressed first went around the corner to get fresh bread for breakfast while the other made coffee. We'd then plan our day around the food we were going to cook. My life was pretty free; I only had a daily French lesson with Marie Helene, my first-floor neighbor. I wonder now what compelled me to learn French while living in Spain. Perhaps it was because the lessons were free, but more likely it was because Marie Helene always had the best gossip. She sat at her door every day, like the Oracle at Delphi, watching the street and catching passing snippets of rumors about the landlady or her priestly son or the neighbor in the house next door.

Martha had a vacationer's schedule during her two-week sojourn. After breakfast she would be off to see her acne specialist. Then in the late morning she would call Pedro at an appointed time to find out if he could get away from work and wife. If it was a thumbs up, she'd come home to let me know and I'd head out to a café, where I'd spend the afternoon with my books and journals, imagining what was happening in the back room. If Pedro was busy, Martha and I would roam the streets and the markets in search of the best ingredients for whatever we were cooking.

Martha knew food and she knew the city. She educated me on both. We'd go across the river to the big market in Triana that never ceased to intimidate me. It was in the old gypsy quarter and, in my first days in Seville, I had been warned by Marie Helene, my landlady, Señora Sala, and others to "be careful around the gypsies. They'll steal the shoes off your feet if given half a chance." So I stepped carefully and purposefully when we got there, but Martha said hogwash to all that, declaring, "If you want fresh seafood, you go to Triana."

On other days we'd meander our way through back streets until we hit the antique market. Busts of heroes and statues of suffering saints lined the street and led the way to the fruit and vegetable market. This was my favorite market in the whole city; each time I walked into it I was instantly and pleasantly overwhelmed by the smells, the colors and the banter between the patrons and the sellers. Everyone had their favorite vendors. Mine were Señor Perez for tomatoes, onions and peppers; Señora Hererra for beets and turnips (she would save me all the lopped-off beet greens, thinking I was feeding hungry rabbits at home); the egg lady for eggs, of course; and finally Martine the potato man, my last stop on market day. He always picked my kilo of potatoes with care, rejecting those that were not worthy of my bag. Then he'd hand it to me, always touching my hand just a little. But the best part of potato shopping was that, as I turned to leave, he would serenade me with *"Vaya con Dios"* every time. It never dawned on me until much later that he didn't sing to other women. His song was probably his way of flirting with me, but I was so timid about such things and didn't believe that someone would want to flirt with me. I never even thought to look back and at least give him a smile. Nevertheless, I ate a lot of potatoes that winter.

There were (and still are) very definite protocols to follow when shopping at any Spanish market.

Rule Number One: when you approach a stall where other people (mainly women) are waiting, you must always ask, "*Quién es la última?*" There isn't a proper queue here so you have to find out who's last in line or suffer everyone's wrath if you go out of turn.

Rule Number Two: never, ever rush anyone or show impatience when it's their turn at the stand. A person's turn is her time to shine—to perform, socialize, ask about the family, tell saucy jokes, talk about the latest happening on the street and, of course, flirt with the vendor in hopes of getting a few more grapes or an extra lemon.

Rule Number Three: don't ever pick up a pear or squeeze a tomato— the displays are for eyes only. The vendors who stand in the center, high above you like wrathful gods, pick and pack the produce for you. You can reject one they pick and ask for another but only by pointing at it carefully without touching the flesh. For heaven's sake, don't pick anything up!

Rule Number Four: smile and say thank you. Vendors will remember you as a good and pleasant customer.

Martha sometimes got away with breaking the rules. Her Spanish was good enough to crack jokes and talk recipes with waiting women and vendors alike. She said she had picked up her Spanish on the streets of New York. Of course, it was Puerto Rican Spanish, but that didn't faze Martha. Unlike me, she was not embarrassed about making mistakes. I had tried to learn Spanish from books and got stuck in the present tense with my American accent for the rest of my life. I just kept my mouth shut when I was shopping with her. If we were in a hurry, Martha would turn on the charm, allowing us to move up the queue. She flirted with the vendors (I kept her away from my potato man) and, at the same time, haggled prices down to a point where she could express gratitude and leave the vendor feeling gracious at his generosity. She always got the best of everything when they filled her orders.

With our bags and boxes, we would head back to my kitchen with its two-burner hot plate and just enough room for the two of us to chop and talk. Martha would say, "Honey, it doesn't matter how many burners you have. It's all about what you cook on them." My first lesson was for *pollo en salsa de almendras,* which sounds a lot more exotic in Spanish than just plain chicken in an almond sauce. While we chopped garlic and onions, the potatoes boiling on the hot plate, Martha told me about Pedro. She had met him five years earlier in the waiting room of her acne specialist. She said that, at first glance, she wasn't much impressed by this short Spaniard, but she figured she wasn't much to look at in that first-glance way either. He was there with a rash and a roving eye. He offered her a cigarette and asked her out to lunch. With all his gold-banded hand holding and leg rubbing, she had lapped up more than her meal that day. When he later proposed that he join her for a siesta at her hotel, Martha told me, "Believe you me, the word 'no' was nowhere close to my lips." That first time they made love she kept her slip on so that he wouldn't see the Statue of Liberty. After that, it didn't matter—they were hooked. Now, every year for two weeks, she comes over for acne treatment and love. Her story was pure romance, a love-in-the-afternoon affair that was oh so European. I was jealous. She told me that now he talks of marriage…if Spain would ever allow divorce. Ah, men!

Once the cooking started the storytelling was suspended until simmering began. She heated oil in my one big pot and added the onions and garlic. She then placed them into a mortar, added pine nuts and almonds to the oil, added that to the mortar, and set me down at the table to pound away with the pestle. While she browned the chicken, I mashed the mixture into a paste with rosemary and thyme. I loved to watch Martha work in that little kitchen. She brought a dignity and passion to browning chicken that I never felt when I did the job. As she splashed white wine onto the browned chicken, then added peppercorns and bay leaf and parsley, she called me back to the kitchen with my paste for my most important lesson of the day—preparing saffron.

Saffron is a very delicate, very expensive spice, and to ruin a piece is to ruin a meal or life or something of that nature, according to Martha. She wrapped a few filaments of saffron in brown paper and held it over the hot plate fire for a few seconds. She said this would make the saffron more powerful. However, you had to be very, very careful—you could easily set it and yourself on fire while you were doing this. She added the saffron and a little water to the pot and set it to simmer. We went back to the dining room to finish the story and the rest of the bottle of wine she'd opened.

Martha was a very pragmatic woman. She didn't have any illusions about living happily ever after in a villa in Seville with Pedro while taking care of her own brood of *niños*. She knew he would never leave his wife and children. What she did have was a healthy dose of the spirit of the 1970s— she enjoyed the moment and thanked Planned Parenthood for her free birth control pills. She was flattered that Pedro had picked her up—acne and all—but two weeks once a year was just fine, at least for now. Years later, I saw that movie with Alan Alda about a couple who meet once every few years just for love and lust and wondered if Martha and Pedro were still meeting. I was telling a friend about it and she said, quite angrily, "It hurts just the same when you're the person at home and you find out." But this was still Seville, in 1974, and I was enjoying this funny woman and her sexy stories of illicit love.

I only met Pedro once, on the day before Martha was going back to New York. She asked me to go on a picnic with them. I think it was a thank-you gesture for giving them a place to make love. She and I prepared the take-along feast: a Spanish tortilla—fried potatoes, lots of garlic and eggs—salad, bread, cheese, olives and bottles of wine. She also wrapped up a bag of sardines with the guts still in them. She was going to roast them on the open fire at the picnic. I told her I wasn't so sure about that, particularly with them not being cleaned out. "You'll love them," she said. "You just have to grill them outside because they stink to holy heaven if you roast them in the kitchen."

When Pedro came to pick us up I wondered what reason he had given his wife for being away from home for the midday meal. He was shy around me; perhaps he was embarrassed, since I'm sure he knew that I had heard all the gritty little details of their romps in the back room. It must have been a little odd for him to play the courteous visitor in a place where he felt intimately at home. But none of that mattered when I saw the way he looked at Martha. It was obvious that he adored her, which made me momentarily weepy in that heart-plucking sentimentality I try to hide within my usual Capricorn practicality.

We drove out of Seville. It was my first trip outside the city limits. Martha sang Beatles songs in the front seat and I joined in. Pedro said nothing for the whole half-hour trip through the countryside. We finally stopped in the middle of a forest laden with large old trees I didn't recognize. Martha said they were cork trees. I had never really thought about where all the corks plugging all the bottles of wine I had opened in my life came from. Now, here I was, standing in the midst of their birthplace. I was humbled by the useful beauty of those trees.

Pedro started a fire and Martha put the smelly sardines on to grill. She was right—they stank to high heaven. The lovers were relaxed and happy with one another and their contentedness rubbed off on me. I spread out our blanket and unloaded the food from the basket. We ate and drank and laughed. Not once did I feel like a third wheel. Then they went further into the forest, where the big pine trees stood, so they could say goodbye to one another privately under the open sky. I didn't mind; I had all these beautiful trees to keep me company. I imagined while I was sitting there that this was the mysterious Andalusian forest where the poet Federico García Lorca was taken out and shot in the early days of the Civil War. I knew the place was actually somewhere around Granada but I liked thinking that his spirit was here with me and Pedro and Martha. When they got back, Martha—ever the teacher—had a handful of pine cones. She built a little fire and showed me how, if you place the pine cone into the fire and turn it occasionally, the cone will pop open to reveal a dear sweet pine nut.

We drove back in silence, everyone sated by sun and food and wine. They dropped me off at home with the pots and glasses and empty wine bottles and then went off to wherever lovers go in the early evening when the roommate is home. I climbed the three flights up to the apartment and unlocked the door. Already it seemed too empty, even though Martha wasn't leaving until the next day. I knew she was probably spending the night with Pedro in a hotel somewhere but she had promised she'd come by in the morning to say goodbye. Being a person who starts to anticipate the pain of loneliness long before the event even happens, I was already sad. I washed dishes and cleaned the kitchen that we had left "as is" when we finished cooking then curled up with a book I didn't read.

Martha must have slipped in when I was in my French lessons at Marie Helene's because, when I returned to the flat, her suitcase was gone. What I did find when I opened the door was her farewell present: food. Bags and bags of food. There were bottles of olive oil and wine; cans of beans and bags of spices, carrots, potatoes and beet greens; and, in my tiny refrigerator, cheese and chicken and fish wrapped in cloth to keep it fresh. She had written down all the recipes we had cooked together and bought all the ingredients for me to carry on without her. On the counter was her final gift to me—a tiny container of saffron with a note saying "Take Care."

A Holy and Profane Fiesta

You Can't Tell the Players without a Program

I didn't want to leave, not really. Seville was everything I had ever wanted in a place to live. I had a great apartment, friends, cheap wine, great food, Celtas cigarettes at the corner and roving seranaders on the weekend. It was perfect. But I had ignored my expired visa long enough that now I was terrified to go to the police and ask "*Por favor, solamente Semana Santa?*" I had a basis for my fear. This was, after all, Franco's Spain, where I felt nervous enough being here legally, let alone with an expired visa. My French teacher-*cum*-neighbor, Marie Helene, didn't help matters, since she always sprinkled dire tales of missing foreigners and dark dungeons in with my French lessons. How could anyone leave Seville before the holy week extravaganza even started? I'd be the only pilgrim on the road leaving as the hoards poured into the city. It was really all too sad.

I went down the three flights of stairs to tell Señora Sala, my diminutive black-clad landlady, that I'd be leaving at the end of the week. I took my passport for a show-and-tell explanation. She looked at the expired visa and then up at me as if I had committed some kind of criminal act, which, in a way, I had. I didn't want to try to explain to her that I was too scared to go to the police to get an extension, believing that they'd just haul me to the border and dump me on the other side. Señora Sala shook her head and made a little "tsk" sound, just once, then pointed to the clock on the wall. "*Un hora, aqui.*" She tried to speak to me in verbless sentences, since she knew I had problems with verb tenses. Then, with a wave of her hand and the one word "*Passaporte,*" I was dismissed.

One hour later we were standing in the police station to plead my case for an extension—or rather, she did the pleading. I just stood by trying to look meek, honest and deserving as I handed over my passport. The two green-uniformed officers behind the counter shook their heads at each other as one of them tapped at the expired date. It didn't look promising. Then I saw Señora Sala shuffle closer to the desk and, looking up at the officers, say something of which all I could understand were the words "*Madre,*" "*Catolica*" and "*España.*" The two policemen almost saluted her as they nodded their heads towards her and then my passport and stamped it with a flourish, with a full-page permission for me to stay in Spain for another two weeks and not one day more. I figured the mere mention of church, mother and homeland in Catholic Spain was enough to clinch the deal. Señora Sala linked her arm in mine and proudly led me away.

Holy Week was always a very significant time in my life. Where I grew up, Holy Week was never actually the whole week but rather three days crammed full of churchly rituals—the washing of the feet, the stripping of the altar, laments and sadness and what seemed like hours spent in church. My father would impose a "no music, no playing, no fighting" rule from noon to three p.m. on Good Friday to mark the suffering and death of Christ. I sometimes wondered how he knew the exact time period that Jesus died, and anyway, wasn't Jerusalem in a different time zone than Columbus, Ohio? Needless to say, I did not voice any of these questions but kept my eyes on the prayer book in front of me and my thoughts on counting down the remaining two days. On Saturday dispensation was always given to my mother to color Easter Eggs, supposedly for the Easter Bunny to put in our baskets. I never doubted that either. For me those three days were all about getting to Easter, when I could sing Alleluias, wear my new hat and reindulge in whatever bad habit I had sacrificed (usually candy or fights with my little brother Tom).

As my father had led my early Holy Weeks in Ohio, my landlady, Señora Sala, took on the role of holy guide for this Sevillian one. Now that I was legal and she and I didn't have to worry about the *Guardia Civil* pounding on the door, she could concentrate on getting me ready for the week ahead. First of all, she sent me down to the *tobaconista* on the corner to buy a five-peseta play-by-play program of the schedule for the week. It was going to be a busy week, since over fifty churches would be sending out their suffering Christ and weeping Virgin statues for their annual jaunt around town. Señora Sala wanted to make sure that I saw the all-stars. She marked my program with the concentration of a hooked bettor picking her numbers for her bookie. In honor of the season, she penned in big black crosses beside her choices.

First, she marked those virgins whose departure from their churches required dramatic feats of strength and tricky maneuverings by the stevedores, who were doing all the carrying while hidden underneath the skirts of the floats. From the blank look on my face, she could tell I didn't understand any of that, so she fell dramatically to the floor. I nodded a *"comprende"* to the excitement of the possibility that maybe this year they'd trip and the holy statues would come tumbling down. After she pulled herself up from the floor, she tapped the program with an emphasis that I took to mean that these next guys were the ones I had heard about, who had a particularly fanatical following either for religious reasons or neighborhood pride. From the seriousness of her look I knew that I was not to miss any of them. Finally, with a smile, she placed two crosses each beside all her sentimental favorites, including the church across the street. I noticed that the bulk of the crosses were from Thursday to Saturday, just like my childhood Holy Week. Then she handed me the program, took off her glasses and tilted her head at me as if to say, "It's up to you now, *chica*."

Let the Games Begin

It didn't take long for me to get wrapped up in Holy Week à la Seville, with or without a program. Early Monday morning when I went around the corner to get my bread, I ran smack dab into my first procession. Coming towards me down the narrow, no-American-cars-would-fit-here street was a life-size rendition of the third Station of the Cross—Jesus Falls the First Time. I knew them all. They were engraved in my memory from the Lenten Friday afternoons when all St. James the Less students would file into church to follow the stations. Did it always get ominously dark with thunder rumbling when we reached Station Twelve—Jesus Dies on the Cross—or was that my imagination? As I stood there gawking at the statues (they were my first, after all) one of the other women pulled me back against the wall where we stood, smushed, allowing room for the six or seven penitents and Christ and Mary to pass. Then, with a sign of the cross, we all moved into the bakery as if nothing had happened.

I was hooked. I started ignoring things like housecleaning and laundry and instead slipped down the three flights of stairs and roamed the streets looking for my next procession. Since all of them had to pass through the Cathedral to pay homage or be judged by the bigwigs or something, I could have just sat with Marie Helene out front of our building and watched them make their way down Mateos Gago, but it was more exciting to roam around and come upon one by chance. Señora Sala hadn't marked any of the processions on Monday or Tuesday, probably signifying that they weren't worth the trek down the stairs to see. This made me feel sorry for them. None of them seemed to have a lot of penitents or crowds watching on the streets. What's a parade without people to watch it? I imagined that these were the working-class churches too poor to attract money from rich penitents or jewel-bearing celebrities. I declared them my personal favorites.

All the processions were basically the same, but that made no difference to me. I have always been a big fan of parades and spectacles of any sort. Since these were religious processions, all were led by the priest, accompanied by cross-bearing and incense-swinging acolytes. As they passed I instinctively made the sign of the cross. It was Holy Week, after all. They were followed by disturbingly KKK-like, pointed-hooded marchers and guys with sack-like hoods over their heads carrying heavy-looking wooden crosses or hitting themselves with straps. My go-to person for all things *Semana Santa*, Señora Sala, told me they wore these coverings so we wouldn't know who was asking forgiveness for some particularly foul deed they had done that year (or maybe they were just getting insurance against one for the coming year). If I were God, I would have insisted that they show their faces in order to get forgiveness. The main attractions came after the penitents, when the floats of the suffering Christ and the weeping mother would pass. Coming up the rear, a drum and bugle corps beat out a dirge to keep penitents and floats moving. When I would run into Señora Sala on the stairs or while we hung our laundry on the terrace, I'd gush to her about how wonderful it all was and would show her in my program the ones I had seen, with or without her recommendation. She'd give me a Mona Lisa smile and say, "*Hasta Jueves*," and leave it at that.

Putting the Holy Back in the Week

As the week passed, it was hard for me to balance the holiness with all the fun I was having running around the city. It was like a big party and I was invited, for once. Flowers were blooming, bars and cafés were filled no matter what the time of day and people seemed to be shouting even more than usual in that loud, slightly threatening way that Spaniards use to talk to one another even when they're smiling. But with all the fun I started to feel a little shame about enjoying myself too much in this holiest of holy weeks. In an attempt to balance my holy week memories in Ohio with those of Seville, I started to visit each of the processional churches to light a candle and say a prayer. My mom had told me when I left on my first trip to Europe that if I lit a candle and said a prayer inside a church

I'd never visited before, my prayers were one hundred percent guaranteed to be answered, or maybe it was fifty percent. I guess she figured I'd be encountering a whole lot of new churches, so my odds of success were even greater. In retrospect, maybe she was hoping that I would be too busy praying and lighting candles to have time for other things that twenty-somethings were doing in the 1970s (unless that's what I was praying for).

When Holy Thursday arrived, Señora Sala knocked on my door (something she had never done before). I stood in front of her, hiding the breakfast plates that were still on the table even though it was well past eleven. "*Hoy Madrugada. Siesta.*" With that, she was gone. I knew from my program what she was talking about. This was the all-nighter, when most of the big hitters would be leaving their churches. She just assumed I would be among the all-night masses, even though in the six months I'd lived here I had never been out past midnight, but maybe that was why she was reminding me to take a nap.

This was also the night when our very own neighborhood church would be sending out its penitents and statues. I thought about inviting Burl and Beryl over—the exotic, irreverent American couple I had met my first week here—since I would have a bird's-eye view of the procession from my laundry-laden top balcony. Here they could see the whole staging of the event, from the incense-swinging acolytes to the last note of music from the band. But then, having been with them at other processions, I knew they'd be judging this one like it was an Olympic event: zero points for creativity, three for costumes, two for musical score. I had laughed along with them at the others, but this was my very own neighborhood procession. I didn't want to combine the profane with the sacred—not this time, not with Señora Sala watching. I told them instead that I'd meet them later for the all-night extravaganza.

I spent the morning getting in provisions for the next couple of days. Señora Sala had warned me with emphasis that *everything* would be closed on Good Friday (my dad would have approved for sure). I felt an urgency to get out and buy, buy, buy. It wasn't food I was worried about—it was wine and cigarettes. As I tripped down the stairs, slithering past Señora Sala's door, I felt an incredible shame that now, at this holiest of holy times of the year, I was anxious about supplying my vices. I contemplated, as I opened the street door, abstaining from both until Easter, having my very own mini-Lenten sacrifice. Wouldn't that be good and righteous? I shamefully went first to the *tobaconista*, having calculated how many packs of Celtas I'd need for the all-nighter about to happen plus enough to get me through Friday. When I got to the bodega there was already a line out the door, making me feel marginally better since, in reality, I wasn't bad, just doing what the natives do. Spaniards can do without a lot of things, but definitely not without cigarettes and alcohol. To convince myself that I really had other necessary shopping to do in addition to my addictions, I also went to the market and stood with all the other women over the tubs of olives, pickled tomatoes and nuts, getting an assortment to nibble on. It was then I made a small vow to myself that I would not smoke one cigarette while my neighborhood procession was in progress.

I decided to dig out my too-warm-for-this-weather black turtleneck to wear, since I had noticed at the other processions that that was definitely the color of choice of those most visible spectators, and since I was going to be on my balcony it might allow me to fade into the shadows. It wasn't the best of processions, but it was mine. As it left the church, I leaned over and could smell the incense as it wafted up three stories to my nose. I thought that if I was home I'd be smelling the same kind of incense while I watched twelve men (always men then) getting their feet washed up on the altar in honor of Holy Thursday. I wondered if that was happening anywhere in Seville tonight. Then the Virgin arrived at the door of the church and my thoughts were right back here. From my perch, I could see the top of her haloed head almost reaching the wires across the street. As she stood there in the doorway a man standing on Señora Sala's tiny balcony below started singing a *saeta*—the lamenting, praising, loving song to this suffering mother. It made me cry. Señora Sala was sitting next to him in her best black dress, mantilla and fan. She looked up my way and nodded her approval that I was there watching. The song ended and the Virgin moved down the stairs, following the rest of the procession down the street away from the Cathedral. Even those churches close by had to make the trek all around the city just to get back home.

A Señora-Sala-Approved Slipping out of the Holy

I made my way across town to meet up with Beryl and Burl. We were going to watch the rock star of all virgins leaving her church. This was the Macarena, the Virgin of Hope, the one everyone in the city wanted to see, so this was the place to be. She had a massive following. Bullfighters wouldn't think of getting into the ring without a prayer to her, promising new jewels and novenas if she kept them safe just one more time. Politicians swore lifelong adoration (and a rich donation to the church) if she'd get them elected. Ordinary folks prayed to her for their health or to get jobs for their kids and didn't promise anything in return, just a "thank you." When I saw the already Times-Square-on-New-Year's-Eve-sized crowd waiting, I prayed to her that my feet would continue to keep me upright and that my overwhelming, claustrophobic dislike of large crowds would hold off until she came out.

I found Beryl and Burl in one of the small bars across the plaza. They already had an entourage around them so decided that they'd prefer to watch the event from there, promising to send out orders of Cruzcampo beer and chips to keep me going while I stood outside the church. I waited for two hours. It seems processions—unlike bullfights—don't always start on time, especially the headliners. But then the doors of the basilica opened and it all began. By this point in the week I had probably seen thirty Virgins or so, but this one truly was spectacular. If I had been judging Virgins by the amount of lace, jewels, crystal tears, candles and flowers they were adorned with, she would have been the clear winner. Shouts of praise for her beauty, compliments, proposals for marriage and just plain love erupted from the crowd; it was a mix of everything from pious adoration to sexual flirting. Legend has it that, years back, a drunk in the crowd shouted profanities at her, horror of horrors, and then threw a beer bottle at her and hit her cheek. It bruised her face immediately (mind you, she is made of wood), but artists were able to restore her to her previous pristine beauty. However, the bruise came back that time and every time since that she has been restored. *Sevillanos* believe that the bruise continues to resurface because she wants the man who did it to always remember his terrible sin. That's why he, his sons and probably his sons' sons walk in self-imposed chains behind her statue every year to ask forgiveness. I believed it all.

I collected the others from the bar and we moved with the throng to other processions that Señora Sala had marked on my program. We were on our way with everyone else to one infamously popular Holy Week plaza. This neighborhood had not one, but two virgins out parading tonight. Señora Sala had included a few stars with the crosses beside these two. We reached the plaza just in time to see them cross paths—one was on her way back home while the other was on her way to the Cathedral. As the two lace-clad virgins made their entry, taunts of abuse poured on each of them from different sides of the place. "Your Virgin is as ugly as a pig," "Your Virgin is a whore" and other words that were definitely not part of my Spanish vocabulary. I felt a little saddened by it all, so as Beryl and Burl continued the night in a *churros* and hot chocolate bar, I made my way slowly back to my place with a sense of the holy still intact.

Back to a Holy Ending

Then it was Good Friday evening. I had decided, or maybe she did, that I would spend this holy night with Señora Sala. Outside, everything had changed. The shops indeed hadn't opened up all day and even the bars were shuttered. There were still huge crowds on the streets but everything was Sunday quiet. I tried to calculate the time to see if it was three p.m. in Columbus, Ohio, but the good Señora was pulling me forward. Even she wasn't talking—with or without verbs—which was remarkable for her. After walking past the Cathedral and down a tiny street on the other side, she stopped and pulled me back against a wall. From my previous procession experience I knew we were setting ourselves up for good viewing, along with the rest of the crowd assembled here. But this was different; as loud and boisterous as the crowds had been last night, this one was as quiet. Hardly anyone was talking and the ones who did were whispering like they were in church. As we stood there more people came, and even as the crowd grew there still was an eerie hush on the street. Then, from around a bend farther down, came the beginning of the procession and the biggest number of cross-carrying penitents I had seen yet. No one said anything as they passed; there wasn't even the tapping of the drum to keep everyone in line, just silence. Slowly they passed, and then, at the rear, the statue of the crucified Christ loomed over us and moved at a crawl past all of us on the sidelines. Not one sound was made from the crowd as it passed. I could hear every footstep and every grunt of the stevedores. *El Silencio* put the capital-H "Holy" back in my week. As it passed, I thought of my dad and those silent Good Fridays of my childhood and understood, here, now, the lesson he was teaching us: that it was good to take a few hours every year to be quiet and remember the blessings of sacrifice that others have made and that we ourselves need to make every once in a while—and not just giving up candy, either.

Off on the Road to Morocco

Beni Mellal, Morocco
April–July 1975

When I wrote to my mother that I was going to Morocco, she replied, "Didn't Bing and Bob go there?" She was, of course, referring to Bing Crosby and Bob Hope in their classic *Road to Morocco* movie from the 1940s. I thank those two and their antics for giving my mother a Hollywood spin on this place so that she could appreciate my adventure without worrying about me quite so much. She didn't have to know that my first day in Morocco saw me unromantically stuffed on a crowded, un-air-conditioned bus with people and chickens and other livestock chugging across an endless-seeming flat plain on the road to Beni Mellal. It was late spring when I started this journey; not the best time to head away from the sea, but I thought that since this town was tucked in the foothills of the Rif Mountains it would probably be cool in the summer. I'm glad I didn't know then what I found out a few short months later or I would probably have turned back.

Unlike most of the other twenty-somethings I encountered in Morocco, I was not here in search of dark dens full of cheap drugs to keep me blissfully unaware of everything around me. I passed a few of those places and, instead of luring me into their shadows, they scared me off to the nearest place I could buy a beer (which isn't always that easy in a Muslim country). And unlike Bing and Bob, I wasn't in search of adventure or romance. I was here because my visa had run out in Spain. That was it. I had to go somewhere and Morocco was a short ferry ride across the Mediterranean—with the added bonus that I would get to see the Rock of Gibraltar, which was high on my list of "Places You Absolutely Have to See in Your Life." And, having cried my way (at least seven times) through the ending of *Casablanca* when Humphrey Bogart looks Ingrid Bergman in the eye and says "Here's looking at you, kid," I thought the mystery of the place might be intriguing. I would bravely leave my European roots behind and live on the exotic side for a while. But none of these is the real reason I chose Morocco; I was here because I had a standing invitation to visit Françoise. Knowing someone anywhere, even if I was not in the least bit interested in that place, pushed that destination high up as a potential home away from home for me. But as the bus took me farther and farther away from Morocco's tourist world, I had my first tremors of culture shock that seemed to grow proportionately with the number of stops the bus made in the middle of nowhere. I started silently chanting my comfort mantra: "Françoise's address is in your pocket. Breathe. Françoise's address is in your pocket. Breathe."

But this wasn't that much of a comfort, to be honest, since I didn't really know Françoise all that well. I had met her and her medical student fiancé, Pierre, in Paris earlier in the year before I headed to Seville. They were good friends of Jacqueline, the girl whose Paris apartment I had stayed at. To tell you the truth, I didn't really know Jacqueline all that well either. My youngest sister's beau, Henry, had met her at a bar when he was in Paris a couple of years earlier during his "American in Europe, Army-Style" days. To hear him tell it, he turned on his considerable charm and mixed in a dose of American brashness so that, by the end of the evening, he had her phone number and an invitation to look her up the next time he was in Paris. But since he was about to marry my sister and didn't think she'd appreciate meeting one of his passing sweeties, he reluctantly bequeathed to me the paper with Jacqueline's number on it as a kind of bon voyage gift.

Jacqueline, being a very properly raised daughter of a high-ranking officer in the French military, took her promises to the armed services of any country very seriously. So when I called and reminded her of the American soldier she had met and could she please recommend an inexpensive place for me to stay in Paris, she responded without hesitation, "My mother is out of town so you can come and stay with me." If I had known the word "gobsmacked" back then I probably would have used it to describe my reaction to the invitation, and that was even before I saw the old, elegant, spacious apartment where she lived. It was one of those typical old Parisian buildings—hers overlooked the Parc des Invalides, where kids played and nannies watched. Inside there was one of those quintessentially European wrought-iron elevators. I had won every American tourist's jackpot of places to stay in Paris. And it only got better.

Every night that I was there I would help Jacqueline cook dinner for crowds of her friends, including Françoise. They would all show up at the door with wine and books and the latest gossip about whoever wasn't there. They would argue politics or art or cinema in French—and sometimes in English, to include me. There was enough wine poured that most nights I felt like I understood every word anyway. It was usually the same group of people, so at the end of each meal they would tie their napkins in different shapes—bows, knots, some like birds—so they'd know which was theirs for the next time. I was quite fascinated. One evening, after more than the usual number of bottles of wine had been consumed, Françoise magnanimously invited me to her wedding celebration at her grandmother's house overlooking the Atlantic Ocean in Biarritz the following week. *"Merci et merci!"* What else could I say?

Francoise's *grandmère*, a white-haired, gracious woman, welcomed me like I had spent every summer of my childhood at her big, white house overlooking the sea, just like the others who were there. And she did it all in absolutely perfect English. I could have kissed her—and probably did! Even if she didn't have this fabulous house on a hill where you could hear the Atlantic crashing below, just the fact that she didn't expect me to speak French made me want to sign up to wash all the wedding dishes and clean the lavatories. But she would have none of that. I was one of the "young people" and we were to have nothing but fun, fun, fun this weekend, and she would be paying for it. Except for Françoise and Pierre, who were staying in the "big house," all of us young'uns headed with luggage, sheets and towels in tow down the hill to the local hostel that *Grandmère* had rented for the weekend for our use. From there we made our way to an elegant local café, where we had sweets and coffee, and then headed off to the sea where a group of hardy souls went swimming in the Atlantic—I was not among them—and then back to *Grandmère's* for a *trés chic* American barbecue.

In the late morning on Saturday we gathered with the grownups on the lawn at the big white house and clapped and shouted as Françoise and Pierre came back from the registry office all newly married. *Grandmère* floated around, making sure everyone was eating and that their glasses were kept filled with her famous champagne punch. (I still have that recipe on a scrap of napkin in *Grandmère's* handwriting. I've never made it but maybe someday I will.) I was in a French heaven. That evening we young ones changed into jeans and warm sweaters and piled into cars. We snaked our way high up into the Pyrenees, higher than the electric lines. We took a torch-lit walk through the woods to a cave, outside of which a Basque couple was roasting a whole goat over an open fire and cooking pots of beans and slicing farmer's bread. Inside there were long, rough-hewn wooden tables loaded with jugs of red wine and squat glasses that could be banged on the table in tune to songs and never broken. The only light was from candles hanging from sconces in the walls and stuck in bottles on the tables. Françoise's brother brought in a wind-up record player and we all danced and drank and ate the night away. As day came up over the mountains, we made our way back to the hostel. While the others slept I caught my very slow train to Seville, with both my memories and Françoise and Pierre's address in Morocco tucked in my pocket.

And so here I was now, standing outside the hospital that Françoise and Pierre called home. Françoise led me through the hospital corridors to a tiny little room with a single bed whose white, iron bars reminded me of the crib that all my mother's babies had slept in. I thought that surely they'd have a nice apartment set aside as doctors' quarters, since they were French, but this was it. Their open suitcases and plastic bags of non-perishable foods took up most of the floor space, but Françoise seemed as happy here as she had at her *Grandmère's* palatial home. She was in love, so it didn't matter what the scenery was, just who was in it. And since she had signed on with Pierre, this, shall we say, basic hospital in Morocco was "it." But I guess they thought it was better than the alternative that awaited them in France: two years of separation while Pierre served out his mandatory military service.

Since the bed was the only place to sit in the room, I settled myself on one edge while Françoise rifled through plastic bags and came out with a Toblerone candy bar and a warm Coke to offer me. I took both. She had been living here for the seven months that I was in Seville, so she considered herself an expert on local culture and proceeded to give me her Tips for Survival. They all boiled down to this: I should fear and distrust anyone who wasn't European, and even some of those if they weren't French. I wasn't sure what category an American would fit into but I wasn't about to ask on my first day, when I desperately needed her help to find either a place to live or the fastest transportation to get the hell out of there. She continued, telling me that—in addition to the usual demands for bribes to get anything done at town hall and the merchants trying to steal every *dirham* they could from your tight-fisted hand—the absolute lowest were the natives, who would throw themselves under your car just to get the insurance money. I told her that I didn't have to worry about that one, since I didn't own a car, but I would tuck the information aside just in case my financial situation got desperate.

I instinctively wanted to challenge everything she said with a righteous monologue on French colonial prejudices, but I didn't know a whole lot about colonialism back then—and besides, I hadn't finished my Toblerone. And the fact was, since I didn't have any street smarts when it came to this culture, maybe I should just listen up and take heed for now and dispel her truths when I had found better ones of my own. I bet Bing and Bob never had to worry about such things. But since I did, I took all of this with me to my own little, white, iron bed, where I lay awake listening to the groans coming from down the hall, either from suffering patients or love-making newlyweds.

Settling In on the Rue d'Amour

In the morning, Françoise bustled me and my stuff out the doors of the hospital and into the friendly *Bonjour*s of a black-skirted priest who was standing beside a loaded pickup truck. Père Richard was all smiles and handshakes as he asked, "*Comment allez-vous?*" Françoise told me she'd recruited his help in finding me a place to live since he worked "on the other side of town"—and with the ridiculously low price range I'd given her, that's the only neighborhood where I'd find a place. Not only had the good Father found an apartment for me, he had scrounged up enough furniture from the garages of his more wealthy French parishioners that I could move in immediately. Now what did I think about that? Françoise had that relieved look of a woman who had fulfilled an obligation that she never really wanted to do in the first place but had enough good breeding to know she had to. Père Richard, on the other hand, just looked pleased that he'd been able to help his friend and me. All I could do was say "*Merci*" and "let's do it." I got in the front seat of the pickup and Françoise followed us in her car.

By the time the truck stopped I knew indeed that I was on the other side of town. There were no palm trees or flowers here and not a European in sight. It seems they also forgot to pave the streets and put down sidewalks in this neighborhood. I noticed a lot of veiled heads peeking out of doorways as the truck came to a halt in front of one of the more nondescript whitewashed two-story buildings I had encountered this side of the Atlantic. I nervously suspected that I was in for a more authentic experience than I had bargained for. Off to one side of the doorless entrance to the house were narrow, spiraling stone stairs with a flimsy wooden door at the top. (I was already imagining someone breaking in and carrying me away.) It opened into what was one of the barest apartments I had ever seen. There was absolutely nothing in this apartment—not a refrigerator or stove or even a hot plate. There were no closets or cupboards, not a shelf to put a cup on. There wasn't even glass in the windows, for heaven's sake, only slitted shutters that were closed, making us all into human zebras. I was not happy. The two of them were oohing and ahhing about what a bargain it was to get an apartment this big for such a price, and it even had a roof terrace! I smirked to myself, betting that Françoise would never live in such a place. That's when I saw it—the squat toilet tucked in a doorless, closet-sized room off the hallway where we stood. No sitting down here to do my business, just a hole in the floor with two pads alongside showing where to put my feet, for good aim, I guess. There was no sink, just a spigot in the wall to wash up afterwards. The tremors of culture shock turned into a full-fledged earthquake. (Years later I read a treatise blaming the sit-down toilet for all the blocked-up, unhappy people in the world. To alleviate the problem, the author suggested, if you weren't lucky enough to squat, to at least sit down on the toilet ramrod-straight with arms to the heavens. Even if that doesn't work, it would be preferable to squatting for me.)

But what could I do? Père Richard and Françoise were already unloading the truck and carrying in my furnishings: a table, two straight chairs, a mattress, a soup pot and one skillet, two dishes, one cup and one glass, two forks, two knives and one spoon (I wouldn't be having anyone over for soup) and a one-burner camping stove. When everything was in place the apartment somehow seemed even emptier than it had before. I wanted to cry and call my mom, but she would no doubt have told me to grin and bear it. After all, Bing and Bob always had to go through tough times to get to the happy endings. I accepted Françoise's offer to take me to buy groceries. It would prolong my being here alone for a little while longer. We stopped by the hospital to pick up sheets and towels and then she was saying "*Au revoir*" and I was home alone—but not for long.

While I was in a little side room unpacking my suitcases and putting my things in cardboard boxes that I had bought at the grocery store, I felt a presence other than mine in the apartment. I certainly hadn't heard a knock or anyone calling out but I knew someone was there. I picked up a loose shoe—where are stilettos when you need them?—and peeked around the corner. There was a tall woman dressed in a maroon *djellaba* opening all the shutters, waving at someone outside and laughing at some joke they had. With the sun now streaming in, she must have decided that things were just too filthy and started dusting my table and chairs. I thought of Françoise's warnings and wondered where my passport and money were at that very moment. Then she saw me and, smiling broadly, she came over and shook my hand. "*Je suis Fatima.*" As if that explained everything and would make me drop the shoe I was carrying.

It turns out she was my across-the-street, two-doors-down neighbor and she wanted me to feel welcome. Père Richard had asked her to look after me since this was my first day here. Then she graciously presented me, one thing at a time, with a broom, a mop, a bucket and a round loaf of bread. They were her welcome-to-the-neighborhood gifts. *Merci* seemed too small a word for such a kind gesture. Then she looked me seriously in the eye and said that I must never, ever buy my bread from the stores, because that filthy stuff was filled with hairs and bugs and who knew what else. Someone on the street had found a fingernail in her bread one morning. No, I was to come to her house every morning to make my bread with her daughter. She would pick me up tomorrow morning at eight a.m. to show me where to buy the yeast and flour and after that I could do it on my own. "*D'accord?*" "*Oui.*" Then she left. I thought it too impolite to ask her how she had gotten into my apartment, since I know my paranoid self had locked that flimsy top door when I came in with my groceries. Maybe she didn't need a key; maybe she was my guardian angel in Morocco.

There was a second visit that first day. (Was I having a Scrooge experience here?) This time I did hear a quiet knock on the door. When I opened it, I saw two beautiful, extremely made-up young women dressed in clothing that was a little more revealing than what Fatima had worn. They waved me down the stairs and into the other door that shared the tiny foyer with mine. They were my downstairs neighbors. Now, how friendly was this! I have lived a lot of places in my life, but never have I had two neighborly welcome-wagon visits in the same afternoon. I smiled as I anticipated telling Françoise how wrong she was about Moroccans. The ladies' apartment was smaller than mine and most uniquely decorated. In the center of the room, dominating everything (well, actually, there wasn't room for anything else), was the widest, tallest red-draped bed I had ever seen in my life. The ladies graciously motioned for me to please sit. Now this was no little white, iron hospital bed that I could just hop on up to, no problem. This was a mountain, a bed worthy of a giant. Every time I got my bum close to the top I'd slide off the smooth, shiny cover and have to start all over again. The girls watched my attempts with puzzled expressions. Finally, they came over and each took me by the arm, then sat me far enough back so I didn't fall off. This gave me a fine perspective to observe the decorations while they were off behind a curtain doing something.

All of the walls around the room were decorated with cut-outs from magazines. There was a pouting Brigitte Bardot, a very red-lipped woman smoking Lucky Strikes, a Breck girl, Jackie Kennedy and a bathing suit model selling Chevrolets. I applauded their ingenuity in finding such an inexpensive way to add a little color to the walls and thought about maybe adopting the idea for my decorating upstairs. It reminded me of a visit I had made to the home of a family my brother knew when he was doing good works down in the hollows of Kentucky. All the walls of the house had been papered with Sunday comics. It was amazing; not only did it give color and something to read, but it insulated their cabin as well. They would have approved of the girls' decorations.

Then my eye fell on the main attraction. Spread over the top of the headboard, so high I had to practically lie down on the bed to see them, were five Playboy bunnies in all their bare splendor. Tiny drops of understanding about my neighbors' occupations were starting to trickle into my mind. I wondered about Père Richard's connection to these women—and what exactly did he think I did for a living? The girls came back with mint tea and sweet cakes and squatted against the wall, watching me with silent stares while I ate. I had never had tea with prostitutes before; it wasn't much different from having tea with anyone else, as far as I could see, except that on this occasion I was nervously trying to avoid staring at the pin-ups.

As I nibbled and sipped, they started having a whispered, intense-sounding conversation that I suspected had to do with the real reason I was sitting here. Finally, they took my arms again, swung me off the bed and herded me to the door. There they performed a kind of charade that involved hand gestures, motions toward my stairs and an empty beer bottle. I was never good at charades and never got chosen for teams once my friends saw me perform. I took this personally and so I decided to declare it a stupid pastime, but just the same I longed to guess right just once. With these ladies, I thought maybe the problem might have something to do with the fact that "sounds like" in Arabic would not be helpful to someone who speaks English. The girls were getting frustrated when the solution finally dawned on me. Being Muslim women, they were forbidden by law to have alcohol on the premises. But since their customers often liked a brew or two they had to keep some on hand or they would lose the business. They wanted to store beer on the steps going up to my apartment and pretend that it belonged to me. (They didn't know what a chance they were taking—I really liked beer.) I smiled at them to show I understood and nodded yes with a *Oui* thrown in for good measure. They hugged me a *Merci* and returned to mumbling something between them, probably about my pitiful skills at charades. I went upstairs feeling at home.

Bread Making, Moroccan Style

Next morning, true to her word, Fatima used her Houdini skills to appear once again in my living room. I started to ask how she did that, but she was already pulling me out the door, down the stairs and across the dusty square to a tiny, doorless shop. I let her take charge since I had no idea how to ask for anything in Arabic. The man behind the counter cut a palm-sized chunk of what I suspected was yeast and filled a small brown bag with flour. I was going to make bread. Fatima linked her arm in mine and walked past my house to hers. When she unlocked her heavy metal door—this seemed to be the material of choice for doors in this area of Beni Mellal, for reasons I didn't want to think about—we entered an oasis. This was where they kept the green on my street. Ever since that chapter on "How the Romans Lived" in my freshman Latin class, I had always wanted an atrium, and here I was standing in one. The space, open to the sky, was filled with wild jasmine and roses and geraniums and plants I'd never seen before. All the rooms of the house opened onto this space, where a very shy girl of about twelve stood. Fatima introduced her as Michelle. Fatima was so proud of the fact that she had stayed in school and learned French that she had given all her daughters French names: Thérèse was at university in Rabat, Simone married in Marrakesh, and the baby, Josephine, was out playing. Michelle seemed to have been relegated to being house daughter and teaching me to make bread.

I had never made bread before, never worked with the magic of yeast. When I was little I would join my mother as she made rolls and coffee cakes, watching the bowl of dough get bigger and bigger until she'd let me punch it back down. I was fascinated then, but not enough to take up the trade later in life. I hoped Michelle wouldn't hold it against me. I felt wholesome, kneeling on a tiny cushion on the floor next to my mentor, and thought of my friend Margaret who had left Washington to go live on a commune in Maryland. She would be pleased that I'd finally left the world of Wonder Bread.

Michelle gave me a small bowl of warm water and motioned for me to put my little paper-wrapped portion of yeast into it. Then she poured flour into her big ceramic bowl and told me to do the same. I watched as she made a hole in the middle of her substantially larger pile of flour and then poured her yeast into it. As in a game of Simon Says, I did the same. Once it was all mixed together—a feat I was extremely proud of—the real challenge came. I watched as she spun small bundles of her dough into little, perfectly round loafs. I knelt up a bit for this step and hung over my bowl, then with floured hands I began to spin that pile of wet, sticky dough with my two palms. What had seemed like a fluid motion in Michelle's hands came off like a jerky pirouette when I did it—and my finished loaf showed it. It was a cute but slightly lopsided loaf of bread and I was overly proud of my first effort. Michelle was amused. She would take my loaf with hers to the oven at the corner of the street and I would pick up my finished bread later. Fatima came back at that point, giving a wide-eyed smirk at my finished product, and handed me a square of white cotton, a needle and two shades of blue thread. She told me I had to embroider a cloth to cover my bread with so that it didn't get mixed up with someone else's. (Here I thought its shape would be a dead giveaway.) When I strutted home that morning I found a six-pack of beer and a bowl of couscous on my stairs, the first payment of what would be many from the girls downstairs for my rum-running, Moroccan style.

Afternoon at the French Hotel with the Peace Corps

Françoise came by occasionally to visit and take me someplace new in her car. I think it was a form of penance that Père Richard issued to her instead of Hail Marys when she confessed her sins. Whatever the reason, it was wonderful to get out of my bare rooms. We'd go off to visit her French friends in their villas hidden behind walls of cedar trees, or up to the park at the base of the mountains where ice-cold water that came down in fast-rushing streams from the snow high up on the mountains was channeled into little pools for hot feet to soak in. One particularly hot day in late May, she took me to the French Hotel to swim. It wasn't really a French hotel, but since the only patrons who frequented the place were French, they took ownership of it. (I think they liked it better that way.) But I put aside my disdain for their snobbishness because it was so pleasant to sit around the pool and sip cold beer with the privileged. Some of them even deigned to speak English with me so I could have a conversation about something other than bread and beer.

On this particular day the French Hotel must have lowered their standards considerably because, in addition to this American, there was a local Peace Corps volunteer having lunch and sipping a gin and tonic. I was shocked! What was she doing here? Why wasn't she out building irrigation systems or showing farmers how to get rid of beetles or at least teaching math in a schoolroom that she had built herself? This did not fit with my lofty image of the self-sacrificing youth giving up two years of her life to go off to save the world while trying to spread the good word that Americans aren't all bad, really. It was only ten years since President Kennedy had sent out the challenge for us to do something for our country; had the message become watered down with gin and tonics in such a short period of time?

Her name was Sarah and she was from Minnesota. In that flat, Midwestern twang she told me that she couldn't wait to get back to sub-zero winters and snow. When I questioned the sanity of anyone wishing for that, she leaned back with her gin and tonic in hand and said, "Wait until you've spent a summer here." It sounded an ominous warning indeed, and it wasn't the first time I had heard it. But Sarah wasn't worried about it anymore. She was at the end of her Peace Corps tour and happy to be going back to Minnesota in a couple of weeks. I already missed her and I didn't even know her. Then she asked me the usual three questions: how did you get here, why are you here and where do you live? When I answered the last one, she laughed, "Oh, the *Rue d'Amour*. That must be fun." This made me feel defensive. Even though I knew what the girls downstairs were up to, I felt protective of them; in my mind, if you didn't live on our block you had no right to be judgmental about their choice of a living. (I felt the same way when I lived in a pretty scary neighborhood in Washington, D.C., and my suburban friends would make negative appraisals of my sanity for living in the "danger zone.") Still, I think I blushed just a little, because it was the first time I had heard my street so called and felt a weird sense of guilt by association. But Sarah was too much into her gin and tonic to notice.

Like Françoise, Sarah had a list of warnings about my living here. When she finished the usual ones—like never shaking anyone's right hand, since that was used for other purposes that had to do with hygiene, *if you know what I mean*—and answering any pleas for alms, no matter what the state of the beggar (I saw signs of diseases there that I thought had been eradicated a century before), by saying "Allah will provide." It seemed stingy to me but I practiced it just the same. Then she came to the one that resonated deep into my imagination and scared me to death: "Put a liter pop bottle in the hole of your toilet to keep the rats out of the house." Rats are the one creature in this world that I cannot abide. My fear of them reaches almost biblical proportions. Even someone talking about rats has me headed for the door. From that day forward, I would have to worry about who was swimming upstream to my second-floor apartment to find lunch. It did not make for regular bowel movements. Sarah was oblivious to my reaction and as she finished her gin and tonic and asked, with that Midwestern how-d'-ya-do friendliness that made me homesick for Ohio, if I'd come to supper on Saturday. I put my initial questions about her dedication to the honorable tenets of the Peace Corps to rest when she told me that she lived on my side of town. I figured the Peace Corps was at least keeping its volunteers among "the people" (but definitely not on the *Rue d'Amour*), even if they did spend their afternoons at the Hotel France.

My doubts returned, however, when Sarah's maid answered the door that Saturday. I felt my high school dream of being like those sacrificing Peace Corps volunteers shaken to its roots. How could she justify having a maid when she was supposed to (at least in my mind) live like the people, not use them? She must have seen it on my face and told me that she took Hafeza in when her husband decided he wanted another wife. There are no expensive divorce lawyers here; as is the custom, all he had to do was turn himself around three times while saying "I divorce thee. I divorce thee. I divorce thee," and voila, just like that he was a free man. Hafeza, on the other hand, was out on the street with nothing, not even her own clothes. So, to keep her away from the establishments on the *Rue d'Amour*, Sarah took her in and gave her a home and a job. My warm, fuzzy feelings for the good works of the Peace Corps were restored once again.

Sarah lived in opulence compared to anyone else I knew in Beni Mellal— except the French, of course. When you walked in the front door, you were in a beautiful, blue-tiled patio that was the base of an open center that stretched three flights up, each level of which was edged by a carved wooden balcony overlooking the ground floor, topped with a stained-glass cupola. I could see Bing and Bob now, running around those balconies, escaping from some sinister, robed bad guy who was always just a level away. Sarah led me up the tiled stairs to the middle floor where her living room was. I thought about Hafeza having to carry supper up those stairs and the dirty dishes back down again and wondered if it was worth the trade-off she'd made. As bare as my rooms were, Sarah's were just as cluttered. Every inch of floor space was covered with either carpets or pillows or those lovely little brass tables sitting on carved wooden legs. She was buying up Morocco to take back to Minnesota. I wondered if it would bring some of this warmth and sun to her winter. (I didn't buy any of these things when I lived there and sometimes am sorry that I didn't.)

Sitting there on Sarah's couch, I heard a loud squawking coming from downstairs. I looked over the balcony and there was Hafeza with a butcher cleaver in her hand chasing a chicken around and around the patio below. When she caught it she said something that sounded distinctly like a curse, put its head on a wooden block and came down heavy, with no mercy for that chicken. The headless chicken, just as the cliché says, ran around for another minute or two with blood spurting out of its neck until it realized that it was indeed dead and then thumped down on the floor of the terrace. I had a pretty good idea of what was being served for supper.

While Sarah and I drank beers and then wine, Hafeza was downstairs plucking that unfortunate chicken, chopping carrots, turnips and onions and whatever else she put into this stew that now sat brewing at my feet on a brazier, sending puffs of steam out of the hole in the clay cone that topped it. The air was filled with the aromas of cinnamon and cloves and other scents that I didn't recognize. Sarah called the dish a tagine. I felt entirely underdressed for this meal, too boring in my shirtwaist. As I followed Sarah's lead and scooted off the couch to lounge over the cushions on the floor, I thought I should have borrowed an outfit from the girls downstairs; it would have been much more appropriate, perhaps accompanied by one of those black belly-dancer veils pulled seductively back as I scooped succulent bits of tagine from the pot with hunks of bread (much tastier than mine). It was the most aromatic, glorious chicken stew I had ever eaten. I silently sang a grace of thanks to the unnamed chicken and to Hafeza for making it possible. My tipsy walk back to the *Rue d'Amour* was in the pitch-black night and I prayed to all my girl saints that its paying customers would be tucked into my neighbors' beds by now.

Summertime and the Living is Crazy

As June hit, so did the heat, and everything changed. Well, not everything; I still went to Fatima's every morning with my chunk of yeast, bag of flour and freshly laundered white cloth, now embroidered with a cross-stitch pattern that read "Ann." (Okay, embroidery is not one of my creative talents!) And the ladies on the street still stretched clean sheets on the dirt every morning to dry their couscous. They would squat beside it, laughing and talking until a dog came along, and then they would shriek like banshees and wave sticks to drive it away—then calmly go back to their conversations. The little kids were still going to the Koran school next to the yeast store and in the morning their monotonous-sounding chants would mesmerize me as I chased flies around the dust-filled apartment. It really became useless to clean, since every afternoon the sky would darken. Each time I'd be fooled into thinking that there was going to be a glorious thunderstorm, but instead of rain, a dust storm would move across the town with lightning and thunder thrown in just to annoy me. Since I had no glass in my windows, I could watch the dust filter through the slats as it filled my lungs and covered everything else in the apartment with a fine film.

The girls downstairs still left me plates of food on the stairs, some of which I questioned the wisdom of eating and so included in my bag of garbage scraps and used toilet paper that went to the dump with me every day. (Squat toilets back up easily when you add paper to them, especially the softer version that our American bums prefer; after having to perform a rather messy plunging, I decided to gather all my bits of toilet paper in a plastic bag and deliver it to the garbage heap at the end of the street.) Fortunately, the dump was right across the street from the oven, so on most days the smell of bread overrode that of rotting bones and used toilet paper. The worst part of going to the dump was the little boys who surrounded me as I walked there, shouting "*Bonjour, madame*" or "Hello, American lady." Since I was the only non-Arabic occupant of this street, they figured that my garbage must have some good stuff in it, so each of them wanted to be the first to go through my bags and see what they could score to sell later to the junkmen at the *souk*. Everything was of value here, it seemed: tomato tins, cardboard boxes (I had to buy the ones I had in my closet), glass jars and plastic bags. Seeing these little guys climb over the mounds of garbage was the beginning of my disenchantment with Morocco.

Sarah left the second week of June. She wanted a slow re-entry into her other life, so she was going to make her way through Spain and France and catch a plane in Paris. (Years later, when my nephew was leaving the Peace Corps in Ghana, he asked me to meet him first at my place in Spain; when he explained that he just couldn't go right back, I thought of Sarah. In his case, he figured that if he told his mother he was visiting her sister she would have to forgive him for not hurrying home.) Françoise came by on a Wednesday and we went to the *souk* together. I liked having someone else with me, especially because getting to the *souk* required us to walk down the "street of meat." I hated the street of meat and always avoided it by buying my meat from the French butcher's shop. At the entrance to the street vendors sold bunches of mint to carry with you as you made your way. I would always buy two to hide behind, for not only was the smell terrible, I also didn't want to see the carcasses of chickens and goats and sheep that swung from the stalls, or the vendors swatting flies away from their unrefrigerated meat with a cow's tail. A mosque stood at the far end of the street of meat and there would always be lepers, blind people and cripples there begging. It broke my heart every time I had to pass them while reciting my "*Insha'Allah*."

The *souk* covered a space that could have been used as the parking lot for the Super Bowl. It was huge and sold everything—including those tin cans I had thrown out the week before. Françoise was there to get spices to take as gifts to her family in France when she went to visit them at the beginning of July (everyone leaves, she reminded me). Men in white *djellabas* sat surrounded by huge burlap bags filled with cinnamon, paprika, and herbs for healing and for casting spells. The sight of these spices was one of the few things that made me regret not bringing a camera with me, or at least having some drawing skills. I could put down my mint when I was in this section of the *souk*, but I never threw it away since I knew I'd need its protection again as I passed by the live goats and chickens for sale on my way to the vegetables. The vegetables were sold from ridiculously huge piles spread out on the asphalt. The prices were all about the same and I never got comfortable bartering them down; I figured they were already so low that it was insulting to me as well as the vendor to make a scene. It sometimes puzzled them, but after a while they accepted my ways. I always wondered how long it would take them to sell these big piles of vegetables and pitied the women in the last town on their route, who would be getting the bottom of the pile. I picked up potatoes, carrots, cabbage, oranges and onions; I had been warned to stay away from anything that you were not going to cook or peel and I heeded this message faithfully. But even my adherence to that rule did not keep me from getting worms.

I'm sure that Bob and Bing never, ever had anything as disgusting as worms. My already rocky relationship with the squat toilet took on a whole new dimension, as suddenly the threat of rats coming up the pipes seemed the least of my worries. I went immediately to see Pierre at the hospital. Before he did anything medical, he was sure to lecture me in his own haughty way on the dangers of shaking right hands and eating raw vegetables, both of which I swore to him I had never done. I thought that his lecture was rather unnecessary and that it smacked of blaming the already-sick victim here, but I said nothing. Then he prescribed medication and told me the good news: that it would take about five weeks to get rid of my little friends.

On the way home from the hospital, I walked slowly down the street through wall-to-wall, open-faced restaurants where big pots of soup were boiling in circles of mismatched chairs and only men sat eating from bowls. That particular day, the owner-chefs seemed to have declared cilantro their herb of choice. The smell permeated the air and my nostrils and sent messages of profound nausea from my aching head to my cramping tummy. I started to run. To this day, I cannot abide the smell of cilantro. Anytime it is anywhere around me it sends the same messages and I immediately develop a sort of memorial cramp in my gut. Needless to say, it has never made its way into any recipe in my kitchen, that's for sure. But, as bad as the cramps had been before, they tripled in power after I took the pills that Pierre gave me. The cure was indeed worse than the sickness. I prayed to Allah and all my Catholic saints to please let these little critters take the express bus out of my gut.

They didn't. Those worms made me suffer through every day of those five weeks of recovery. To make matters worse, as if they could have been worse, the temperatures rose—proportionately, it seemed—with my discomfort. I had never experienced heat like this before in my life. The word hell was ever-close to my thoughts that June. And it wasn't long into the unbearable heat that crazy things started to happen.

A Girl Can Only Take So Much

I had started going over to Fatima's in the afternoon, purportedly to improve my embroidery skills but really to get out of the dust and heat of my apartment and enjoy the cool of her oasis. On this occasion Michelle was home alone and sat looking at me sheepishly, even though for the past two months we had been bread buddies and could communicate in our limited ways. She wasn't my embroidery teacher, so she didn't quite know what to do with me while her mother was out. So she did what any good Moroccan would do: she made mint tea. Fatima came rushing in while I was sipping and sat down close to me. She was definitely too excited for this to be about embroidery. After sending Michelle out of the house, she sat down and told me that I had to be careful going out after dark because the mysterious half-horse, half-man was back at it again, going around stealing women to take back to his cave for winter fun. I didn't laugh—at least, not out loud—but she must have read it in my expression. She said, "This is serious. Last year one of the girls on this very street was taken, never to be seen again. Be careful."

A couple of nights later I was walking back from the French Hotel, where Françoise and Pierre had treated me to dinner as their going-away gift. Everyone was going away, it seemed—or at least, the Europeans were. It was dark, very dark, and there wasn't anyone out—the Moroccans had taken this roving Romeo very seriously. As I walked, I felt rather than saw someone following me. This was crazy, I knew, and I shouted "Boogaboo!" which is my word of choice to disperse lurking evils. I didn't hear any reply but I started to run just the same, which was a feat in itself in that heat. Later that night, as I lay sleepless and hot in the dark, I contemplated the positives that might come from life in a cool cave with a lover who was out roaming every night. Then I heard it: the distinct clip-clop of a horse's hooves coming down the street. They stopped just outside my windows— then, as I felt the first needles of that delicious, tingly fear I used to get when my brothers would sneak up on me in the dark, I heard the horse part of the partnership neigh up at my shutters. Hair was standing up in places I didn't even have hair. I wanted to run to Fatima and tell her "I do believe, I do believe!" but that would have meant going outside and I wasn't about to tempt fate that much. I couldn't even work up the nerve to go to the window and take a look at this equine lover. When I didn't show up, I guess he got bored or maybe disappointed, since I heard a little neigh and then a slower clip-clop as he made his way down the street.

By the first weeks in July, everyone I knew outside my neighborhood was gone and the heat just got worse. The street noise, which was so loud in cooler times that I wore wads of toilet paper plugging up my ears, intensified as the temperature rose. I think maybe people were trying to get above the heaviness of the day. And the din started earlier and earlier so that by the time I went to get my yeast in the morning the hawkers were already out there, shouting out their bargains for pots and pans and needles and thread, and beggars with tambourines were starting their days in the dusty little square.

As the heat and the noise picked up, so did the craziness. One afternoon, after I had finished the last of my English books and immediately tried to forget it so I could get excited about reading it again, I heard more than the usual commotion coming up from the street. I opened the shutters (I did not throw up the sash, since I didn't have one) and saw a bunch of little boys—I counted fifty-seven of them—just below my windows. They were screaming and shouting at one another. I recognized some of my comrades from the garbage-dump walk among the group. At first I thought they were throwing a rock back and forth, and then one of them started to swing a terrified cat around and around over his head, which made the others howl even louder. I screamed down in English at them to stop but their din smothered my attempts. I started down the stairs but the girls stopped me, knowing that I would become the next victim of the gang's taunts. I went back upstairs and cried and prayed that they would soon tire of their sport and let the cat survive.

Every day I thought about leaving. There was no reason to stay—just my adherence to an unwritten rule that I would stay in a place for the extent of my visa. I had another month to go, but I thought if July was like this then August would be unbearable. Then the final straw landed on my already-bending back. It was a normal morning; I went over to Fatima's like always to make my bread with Michelle, who was starting to smile more and I think was happy for my company. I just enjoyed the relative coolness of the patio and started to take longer and longer to make my little loaf. I always offered to help Michelle but she always would smile a polite no. This particular morning Fatima had been out, but came in and bolted the door after her. She said something to Michelle that sent her hopping off to the staircase that led to their roof, and then she turned to me and said I couldn't go home just yet. Now, I liked being there, but to be told I was a prisoner didn't sit well with me at all. I mean, I grew up in the land of Life, Liberty and the Pursuit of Happiness, for goodness sake. Then I heard the shouts—or roars, more like—just outside the door, and Fatima motioned me up the stairs that Michelle had taken.

We had a bird's-eye view from Fatima's roof and I could see hundreds of people shouting something to a man who, at that very moment, was bashing in the door to the girls' apartment downstairs from mine. No one was trying to stop him. In fact, they were encouraging him and handing him tools to help with his hammering. He soon broke inside, which built a frenzied anticipation in the crowd. When he appeared again, he had a young woman by her hair, and he dragged her out of the house and down that crummy dirt street, surrounded by the sounds of whooping, whistling and righteous shouts from the crowd. It was the most horrific event I had ever witnessed.

I found out later that the man was the pimp from a house down the street and had found out that one of his girls had gone off to Marrakesh with a customer. Freelancing was not allowed, evidently. When the girl came back she hid with my neighbors, hoping she could escape before he came around again. She didn't. Fatima walked me home that day and I was sickened by the smiles and laughter of the people lingering on the street, retelling the story and probably discussing what great entertainment it had been for this hot morning. The door to the girls' apartment was totally bashed in, but they were all right. I went upstairs and started to pack.

The next morning when I woke up, I felt a perfect bald circle at the back of my head. When I got back to the States, a doctor said it wasn't ringworm—my first thought, since their cousins were just about out of my body and I figured they'd told all the other members of the species what a good host I was—but was caused by stress and anxiety. I went out that morning and bought a ticket for the express bus to Casablanca leaving in a week; I wanted a direct route in air conditioning and non-stop escape from this hell. I went to see Père Richard to tell him I was leaving and let him know when he could pick up the furniture. He was sad, maybe because this left him the only foreigner on this side of town. When I went to Fatima's to make my bread that last week, Michelle didn't smile at me like she usually did. I think she was missing our mornings together already. The girls invited me downstairs for a beer and those sickly sweet cakes of theirs. They cried behind their broken door, though I'm not sure if it was because I was leaving or for the loss of their beer protector. On my last night, Fatima and her family had me to dinner. As a going-away present, Michelle painted paisley swirls on my feet and hands with henna. It was her way of saying "remember me." It was still there when I went through customs a few weeks later, with an extra bag of henna packed so that I could do touch ups. The customs agent, thinking he had scored a big one, asked me, what was that green leaf stuff in that bag? I answered henna. He asked me what that was. I swung my foot up on the counter and said, "That's henna." He let me through. It seemed an appropriate ending to my Moroccan journey.

Annie's Odyssey

Loutraki, Greece
March–October 1976

Starting at Alpha

It took me weeks of wandering up and down the stony countryside to find a true home in Greece. When Odysseus was roaming around, he at least knew where home was. He also spoke the language and had someone to carry his luggage. I wasn't even able to read the alphabet, let alone speak the language. I had learned the capital letters once when my sister and I were coerced into joining the Beta Sigma Phi Sorority for Secretaries (actually it was for a bunch of other females too, but in our chapter we were all secretaries). I didn't want to join, but the president of the local chapter was my sister's best friend from high school and our ride to work every day, so the pressure was intense. It wouldn't have been so bad, but we were working on the university campus, where other girls our age were members of the real white-pillared sororities. Like them, we, too, had a rite of initiation, but the only part I remember of this was that we had to learn the Greek alphabet, capital letters only—symbols and sounds—and pass a test. At the time I wondered why anyone in Columbus, Ohio, would ever need to know the Greek alphabet, but I silently thanked those sorority sisters now for enabling me to at least read the signs in capital letters as I stuttered my way through Greece.

All this wandering began at the end of March when I boarded a ferry in Brindisi, Italy, to cross the Adriatic Sea towards Greece. It was good to be back on the sea again, smelling the salty air and feeling the spray on my face as I stood by the railing watching Italy disappear. That's where I found my own little Hermes (minus the winged feet) to lead me into Greece. "*Ich Demitrio*s," the guy next to me said, pointing to his chest. "*Guten Tag. Ich bin Ana*," I answered, proud of my marginally better use of the German language. That established, he began the saga of his young life. Did all Greeks revert back to their Homeric roots when traveling on the sea? He had left home four years before and traveled to Germany, where he worked for Siemens in Dusseldorf making something I couldn't decipher. "*Viele Deutsche marks*," he smiled as he rubbed his fingers together. That, I understood. Evidently he had made enough, because here he was about to go home and ask his own Penelope to marry him. He was coming home in triumph, laden with full pockets and marvelous gifts to prove his undying love—a refrigerator, a stove, a washing machine and a vacuum cleaner. The sweetness of his tale made me misty. I'm such a sucker for other people's romance.

Despite his four-year absence from his love (and what I imagined should have been a pretty healthy sexual urge to get home fast), my little Hermes did not abandon me when we arrived in Igoumenitsa, a nondescript place on the northern coast of Greece. No, instead Demitrios whisked me from the ferry towards the city. "*Kommen haus*," I took this to be an invitation home. I was worried he had misunderstood my own brief saga of looking for a home here in Greece and decided to adopt me. "*Nein, nein danke*." I didn't mean it to sound so frantic, but from the look I got from Demitrios I knew I had insulted his hospitality. What could I do? "*Eine nacht, bitte*." "*Ja, naturlich*," he smiled back at me, with a promise that he would take me to a town the next day where he was sure I could find a place to stay. This was certainly Greek-hero material and if I could have translated that into my bad German I would have told him so.

Demitrios proudly showed me where his town was on my map. It didn't look all that far from Igoumenitsa, but little did I know that nothing moves as the crow flies in Greece. The bus climbed out of the city, up up up until there was nothing around but scrawny pines, white stones and deep, straight drops to endless valleys. I really should never take the window seat on buses since I tend to conjure up imaginary dangers just up ahead and out of sight. As the driver weaved around the blind curves at high speeds, I kept a prayer to St. Christopher on the tip of my tongue.

Finally we descended the hills and arrived at Demitrios's town, where there was drizzling rain falling and all those mountainous peaks had disappeared into the mist. When I looked out the window of the bus I counted seven houses, a bar, a church and, from the array of brooms, bags of beans and old men sitting in front of it, what looked like an old-fashioned general store. My stomach was reminding me that it was suppertime and when was I ever going to put some food into it. But it would have to wait. Demitrios first had to have a proper hero's welcome home. As he descended from the bus he was surrounded by what surely was the whole town. Someone from the bar came out with ouzo and glasses and, in spite of the rain, an instant celebration broke out right there on the street. I was ignored, except for the ouzo. I wished I had some olives to go with it. Finally, after enough back slapping and ouzo drinking, Demitrios picked up his packages and motioned to me to follow him up a little dirt road that led away from the action. I was starting to get a little anxious.

My anxiety was in full bloom when we stopped in front of a homestead that brought back memories of the Beverly Hillbillies. In the yard there were goats and sheep and a couple of dogs roaming around. I tried to avoid stepping on any of the livestock and keep up with Demitrios but I kept tripping over junk. Demitrios made a beeline for the door and headed inside, where I assumed his Penelope was waiting. I could do nothing but follow him up the steps and into the house. I imagined myself as one of those doomed women in the Greek tragedies I'd read at Ohio State. Inside there was no Penelope—maybe she lived in another town or it was bad luck to see her on the first day—just Demitrios's suspicious mother who eyed me up and down in that distrustful you-stay-away-from-my-son way that I had encountered elsewhere in my travels. I wanted to tell her I was totally innocent and still mending my own broken heart but instead I just smiled.

Two men I recognized from the welcoming committee came in, and we finally sat down to eat. I wasn't sure what the meat was floating around in the plate of oily sauce and tomatoes, but I figured it was probably a cousin of one of those goats or sheep out there in the yard. I had never eaten either and thought momentarily of just smiling and saying "*Nein, danke,*" but I knew that no matter what culture you were living in you should never refuse an offered meal. I swallowed everything whole so the taste wouldn't linger too long in my mouth.

At bedtime there was a loud discussion that included many glances my way—not all of them friendly, but perhaps I just didn't know how to read Greek body language. Finally, Demitrios said I'd be sleeping in his parents' bed—I sure hoped it wasn't with them. When he showed me the bedroom it was obvious that the décor was provided by Demitrios's many packages from Germany. It reminded me of a room I had once in a *gasthaus* in the middle of the Black Forest, although this house did not come close to that German standard of cleanliness. When I pulled the blanket back on the bed I could tell those sheets hadn't been changed for longer than I cared to think about. I decided my ferry clothes were marginally cleaner than the sheets and added a layer of shirt over the pillow, just in case. That night I added two entreaties to my goodnight prayers: Please God, let nothing creep up the legs of my jeans and bite me in the dark, and please, keep my bladder quiet so I don't have to get up in the middle of the night in search of the outhouse.

True to his word, early the next morning Demitrios and I boarded another bus for the seaside town of Parga. Upon our leaving, his silent, suspicious mother handed me a bottle of olive oil as a goodbye-slash-welcome-to-Greece gift. Briefly, the warning about Greeks bearing gifts passed through my mind, but I shrugged it off. The bus headed through the valley and towards the sea that I could see in the distance. It made me smile just to know that it was there and I was going that way. The bus driver did that grating thing with his gears as we made our final descent down into the town of Parga.

When I got off the bus I felt like I had slipped into a scene from *Zorba the Greek*, minus Anthony Quinn. There were little fishing boats rocking in the water and the overwhelming, pungent smell of the sea. I thought that surely this would be a good place to call home. Demitrios pulled me away from my musings and the port and headed up a little hill to a hotel, where his cousin worked at the front desk. The sign over the door said HOTEL ACROPOL, which I could read and pronounce since it was all in capital letters. It was a little two-story white building with a tiny balcony outside the second floor window. I hoped that that would be my room for the night. Inside there was no one around, so Demitrios banged down on the little bell on the counter again and again until finally a sleepy, ruffled-looking man came out from a door on the opposite wall.

He had all the markings of someone who had spent a long night carousing. This was Cousin Alexander. He and Demitrios exchanged a few back slaps and hugs and then we got down to business. I asked him, in a mix of English and bad German, "*Ich*," pointing to myself just in case he didn't understand, "want *zimmer mit kuchen*." He looked to Demitrios for clarification. I assumed the correct translation was given because now Alexander was all smiles and head nods. He turned to me and said, "Sleep hotel," pointing to the floor in case I wasn't sure if it was this hotel or another. "*Haus kommen abend heir,*" more pointing from me to the desk this time. I was confused. Demitrios, being used to my perplexed looks, translated, "*Frau mit kuchen hier abend.*" Ok that cleared up the *reason* but not the *timing*. Did Alexander mean "*abend*" as in late afternoon or early evening, before supper or after supper? When did *nacht* begin and *abend* end? I'd just have to start showing up about six and hope for the best. Now that his charitable work was finished, Demitrios said goodbye to me so he could finally enjoy being home again. Before leaving me on my own, he told me he'd return in two weeks to take me back to the village for Easter celebrations. I thought I heard a Greek chorus of warning.

After dumping my stuff in a tiny room (not the one with the balcony) and checking the sheets (very clean), I set out to explore the town. I always enjoyed that first walk around a new place, seeing it fresh before any kind of good or bad experiences could color it. I decided to start at the sea and make my way up and around and then back to the sea again—that way I wouldn't get lost. My overall impression was that everything seemed to be in need of a good whitewashing, but my perception could have been colored by the steady drizzle that had started to come down. The more tiny streets of gray houses I walked by, the more depressed I got. It took me less than an hour to walk around the entire town of Parga. This was not good—I needed a place to be just big enough to have streets where people didn't know who I was or where I lived. From the looks that I got from every doorway and window, I knew that in this town that would be impossible.

What would I do? I made my way back to the port and sat on a wall to think by the sea in the now-chilly drizzle. The longer I sat there, the deeper I sank into a full-blown blue funk. This was not good, especially on the first day. But one thing I had learned in my travels was that if things didn't seem right it was okay to change my mind. I made my decision: I'd stay through Easter and then head south. All I had to do was find someplace to sleep and cook for the next three weeks. As the sun started to sink I figured it was surely *abend* by now, so I headed back to the Hotel Acropol. Evidently my *abend* did not coincide with Alexander's, because he was nowhere around. I settled myself in the tiny hotel bar with cigarettes, a book and a beer and waited. Not only did Alexander not show up for all the *abend*, he never made an appearance even when I knew we were well into *nacht*.

The following morning, as beams of sunlight shone into the lobby of the hotel, Alexander came to the door with smiles and apologies…at least, I think they were apologies. A tall, skinny blonde (I could tell by her bell-bottomed jeans that she was not Greek) accompanied him. She was Brigit, a German single mother who had settled in Parga a year before. I could have kissed her tiny sandaled feet when she started speaking to me in understandable English. She told me she had a room in her house and I could cook in her kitchen. I thought of Dubrovnik and sharing that tiny kitchen with Frau Sofia and absolutely knew that I could handle any peculiarities Brigit might have about cooking, cleaning and vices (she was smoking, so I knew I'd be okay on that front).

Brigit was the strongest skinny woman I've ever known. She heaved my two suitcases and backpack of books into her tiny car and I scrambled into the front seat beside her. We drove down to the port and then up the hill to a row of tiny white houses that sat perched like seabirds on a precarious-looking path above the port. I had missed these on my walk. There was only a little stone wall separating us from a dreadful fall to the crashing sea.

My vertigo made me vow never to come home after dark (and certainly not drunk) while I lived there.

I would learn many practical lessons from Brigit. The first was taught when we reached the front of her house—a tiny, one-floor, whitewashed box. She tried the door (which I noticed she had painted red just to be different). It was locked. Then she started pounding on it like the sheer force of her knuckles would open it. No luck. She switched tactics, shouting motherly threats for her son to come and open the door. *NOW.* Nothing. "*Scheisse.*" That was the only "bad" word I had learned in German. Brigit then turned to me and explained that her son had left the house, locked the door and taken the only key with him. But she was not to be stopped. With her hands on what should have been her hips, Brigit stood in front of one of the two tiny windows that flanked the door. After measuring the distance between the bars with her hands and giving a satisfied grunt, Brigit stuck her head between the bars and, thankfully, pulled it out again. She explained to me that if you can get your head through a hole you can get your whole body through. I doubted this until she proceeded to test that theory right in front of me. Little by little—first an arm and shoulder, then her head, then the other shoulder and a shimmy of hips, legs and finally those tiny feet—she pulled her body into the house. I applauded her efforts. I wondered aloud if it would work on, shall we say, a slightly more endowed figure. "Your head is the biggest bone. If it goes through, why not the rest of you?" she answered as she unlocked the door for me.

Brigit refused any money for the tiny back room of her house. She said she had enough of that. What she did need was some help painting and fixing things up around the place and planting a garden. I loved to barter. We shook hands on it, just to make it official. When the drizzly rain finally stopped a couple of days later, we began. Brigit dragged all her wooden chairs and the little table we'd been eating at out onto the street. She had cans of blue, red and bright yellow paint for us to use—no grey was going to be allowed in her house. I was given a free hand to do whatever I wanted as long as it was fun. I painted the seat of my first chair red and then alternated the three colors on the spindles at the back. I thought it fit right in with Brigit's hippy style. While we worked her son, Gerhardt, would bounce in and out, busy with his own eight-year-old adventures. This mother and son made a nice pair; they were free spirited but sensible at the same time. I liked that about them.

Lessons in Food and Language

The most delicious food I found in Parga was the yummy, thick goat yogurt. It was even better than the homemade yogurt my commune-friend Margaret used to make when she'd visit me in Washington. She'd travel from Maryland with her yogurt culture packed next to her tie-dyes—it was all very "in" at the time. After tasting the Greek goat yogurt, I was hooked. I thought those goats should have formed a union so they'd never be slaughtered for eating. The yogurt was that good.

Brigit decided one day to teach me how to make tzatziki; she also decided it was time that I went by myself to the only store in Parga where they sold the real stuff that came from the local goats. I had a general idea where it was, having gone with her, but she made me a map to follow just in case. There were no street names on it. I noticed this about map making on my journey; locals never used names, just landmarks, like statues of saints or their cousin's house.

The yogurt store, which was situated all by itself at the edge of town, probably to be closer to those goats, reminded me of the dairy building at the Ohio State Fair. Everything inside was white tiled and sanitary (or at least, so it seemed to me). There were glass-fronted display counters filled with butter, cheese and, of course, the yogurt. As I stepped up to the counter I recited the phrase I had practiced while I walked down one hill and back up another to the shop. "May I have one yogurt, please." I got nothing but a flip of the head backwards from the vendor. I tried again, this time smiling while I said it. Again, the head thing. I thought this flip very rude and probably would have cried but the man finally said, "*Oxi*," with a smile. Now, to an English-speaking person this word comes out sounding a bit like "Okay," but he just stood there. I was totally perplexed. Finally he pointed to the empty space where the yogurt should have been and I understood. He didn't have any yogurt; that's what he had been trying to tell me all along. I had just learned two lessons: if you want fresh yogurt, get there before noon, and even more important, there is more than one way to say no in Greek.

The next day I went back first thing in the morning and got the yogurt so Brigit could give me that lesson in tzatziki making. She emptied the whole half-kilo container of yogurt in cheesecloth and tied it over the faucet in the sink to let whatever liquid remained drip out. Then she sat me down to chop what I thought was an obscene amount of garlic and cucumber.

I mentioned this to her but she shrugged this off with a "What would you know about it?" look. When the yogurt had dripped to her satisfaction, she mixed everything together and smeared some on a piece of bread for me. I was in heaven. If anything, tzatziki made that yogurt taste even better. Brigit informed me that my next lesson was going to be roe eggs. I thought the term was a needless duplicating of the word but soon found out that she actually meant deviled eggs with the salty fish roe mixed in with the yolk and mayonnaise. When, later in my stay, I made and tasted their fishy goodness, I knew that they would never be a hit at one of my family's picnics.

A couple of days before I was to head back to Demitrios's village for Easter, Brigit introduced me to two German friends of hers who were traveling through Greece and were willing to take me as far as the Peloponnese. They said they had enough room for me and my stuff, so why not? By this point in my journey I was a lot more comfortable with the free-wheeling ways of the 1970s but, in spite of the lessons that Suzie had demonstrated in Amalfi, I was still a little shy about going off with two men on a trip that just might involve an overnight stay somewhere. Brigit and the boys were waiting, so I just said yes and thanks and believed it would all be okay. We would leave the Monday after Easter.

To celebrate my imminent removal from Parga, I spent the next day exploring some of the little coves along the coast behind Brigit's house. This coast looked a lot like the one around Dubrovnik. Scrub brush and wind-blown pine trees tried valiantly to get a grip on the stone. I thanked them for at least giving me something to grab hold of as I tiptoed my way down to the water. My precarious footing wasn't helped any by the fine drizzle that was dripping down my neck and saturating my shoes into soggy swamps. I should have turned back then, but I didn't. As I inched my way down the rocky path, the drizzle was giving a good impression of a genuine rain storm, with wind thrown in just to challenge me more. I finally made it to the rocks edging the water and scooted over the exposed rocks to get a better look inside a cove. It only takes one false slippery step to end up in the sea. That's exactly what happened to me. Soaked and sore, I struggled back up the hill to home. By the next day I had the makings of a first-rate miserable cold. Brigit nursed me with mustard plasters and foul teas and told me to skip Demitrios's Easter. But I couldn't. He had been my Hermes when I needed one. I had to go, cold or no cold.

So on Saturday morning I was making my way on foot down the hill to meet Demitrios. I had hoped that he had forgotten but, alas, there he was waiting and waving for me to hurry since the bus was leaving. I really didn't want to go. I felt I had had my Margaret Mead experience the first time I was there. I really didn't need to spend two more days in that little town, with his family...well, I got on the bus. I told Demitrios I absolutely HAD to be back on Sunday afternoon, since my ride was leaving on Monday. He shrugged and said something which I interpreted as "No problem." I would soon learn another valuable lesson: never assume that someone who speaks poorer German than you do understands what you're saying.

The first thing I saw when I walked into the littered backyard was a goat roasting on an open fire—I thanked the gods I didn't have to be there for the slaughter. On the back porch, a young woman I hadn't seen before was washing out what looked the goat's intestine—lunch? Starry-eyed Demitrios told me that this was his Penelope, whom he had married the week after he came home. He pulled her away from the intestine cleaning and into the house, beckoning me to follow so she could show me her hope chest. Does anyone in North America keep a hope chest? The whole idea seems crazy in a world where fifty percent of marriages end up in divorce. Perhaps the hope part is that yours will be in the other half that stays together. I remember when my older sisters graduated from high school the Lane Furniture Company sent each female graduate a miniature cedar hope chest, just to start their dreaming about the real thing. While Demitrios had been making refrigerators or light bulbs or whatever he was doing in Germany, Penelope had been tatting and knitting lacy edges for her sheets, pillowcases and towels and intricately embroidering tablecloths and napkins. They were beautiful.

Unfortunately for me, lunch was tripe, liver, kidneys and whatever else they could extract from the goat. It was all mixed with spinach and, though I tried to hide it all under mounds of yogurt, my mind wouldn't let go of the fact that I was eating innards. When I was little I hated liver more than corned beef and cabbage, but I couldn't leave the table until I had eaten it. I'd smear two pieces of white bread with as much Oleo as I could and press the liver down in it, hoping to camouflage the taste as well as the smell, which always made me gag. Oleo never worked to hide the innards of my childhood and neither did yogurt at this Greek lunch. I couldn't help myself. Some things I just didn't like. An old boyfriend once told me that I had provincial tastes and would never make it in the wider world. I wanted to tell him now that I was doing fine in the wider world, even though I still didn't like innards.

After lunch, everyone disappeared. I assumed they were off taking a nap someplace, which sounded inviting to my still cold-infused body, but no one had assigned a sleeping area to me. I thought about wandering in the rain out to where the goat was roasting to tell her not to take my distaste for her innards personally, but decided instead to pull out paper and start a letter to Mom. For the rest of the afternoon and evening I wrote and read while the others came and went, doing whatever one did on the night before Easter. I offered to help Penelope with the dishes but she just blushed.

Finally, when I was ready for bed, the bells of the church started banging and we headed down a dark and rocky path to the village church. I'm the only one who tripped. Were they all as cloven-footed as the goats? The whole town was there waiting as the priest came out of the church with three lit candles held high over his head. People pushed and fought to be the first to get their candle lit from the mother lode. When someone was successful, huge hurrahs rippled through the crowd. When everyone's candles were lit we marched around the outside of the church singing. Every once in a while we'd all stop and the priest would read something from the big leather-bound book a much smaller man was carrying, or someone would set off fireworks far too close to my ears. We never actually went into the church at all, which seemed strange to my Roman Catholic upbringing. After the candles had been blown out, everyone was given a red egg. (I found out later that the red symbolized Christ's blood dripping down from the cross. I'm glad I didn't know that then.) Before I knew it people were smashing my egg with theirs. I'd get another one and they'd do the same thing. I thought it a little mean-spirited until I figured out that if you held your egg a certain way no one could break it. Ah, physics. By the time we headed back up that goat path I was faintingly hungry, thinking that surely the roasted goat was going to be sliced and consumed. But no, all we ate before bed were the eggs…just those lousy, red, boiled eggs. If I could have cursed the gods in Greek I would have at that point.

Easter Sunday morning, nothing happened. We didn't go to church, nor did we eat. I wondered, why exactly had that goat been slaughtered? Could it have been for a sacrifice to some god or the other? When I thought my boredom and hunger could not endure one second more, the table was set and the roasted goat appeared.

Cold.

They served it cold.

After a day of smelling those mouth-watering roasting aromas, they served the thing cold.

I started to get nervous about getting back to Parga. I looked at Demitrios and tapped my watch—he ignored me. There was nothing to do but just eat the cold goat (which I have to admit was pretty tasty), let my empty glass be refilled and scarf down enough bread to absorb the wine.

We finished about two thirty in the afternoon. While the ladies washed the dishes I followed Demitrios outside and asked him how I was going to get home. He replied, "*Kieine autobus Dienstag.*" Now, I knew that *Dienstag* was certainly not Sunday. I mumbled, in the best outraged voice I could express in German, "*Was?!*" He just gave an irritating shrug that meant the same in any language—what's the big deal, chill. "But you promised," I said. The shrug again. I was moving towards the edge of hysteria. "*Montag, gehen mit Deutche.*" Nothing. No response.

In a huff, I picked up my backpack and my wadded Kleenex and said I'd walk back to Parga. As I was tripping disheartened through the junk-strewn backyard, Demitrios came after me. I had hoped that he came to tell me he would find me a ride and he'd still be my hero. But all he said was that his mother, who was watching grimly from the porch, wanted money for that bottle of olive oil she'd given me on the first visit. I fought back tears as I took what I thought would be enough drachmas out of my pocket to satisfy her and threw them at him in a gesture appropriate for this Greek drama.

I am a take-charge kind of woman when the situation dictates it—my mother called it my bullheadedness. Whatever it is, it provides me with a no-turning-back attitude, no matter how stupid the decision. If I had stopped to really consider what walking in the rain for hours with a head cold sinking to my chest would do to me, I probably would have sat down in that yard and cried. But I didn't. I was soon on the road, shuffling foot after foot and hoping for a miracle. I almost convinced myself that after being painfully bored, half starved and stuck in that little town for a day and a half, the walk would be a welcome escape to be enjoyed. Wrong again.

I started singing to keep my mind off my hurting chest and dripping nose. First, I sang all the songs I could remember that had the word "blue" in the title, and then those with "love" and "heart." When I was finished and looked at my watch, less than an hour had passed. But I was not discouraged. I had a wide repertoire of tunes in my mind, thanks to my family. Every evening in the summer we would sit on the front porch swing to escape the hot house and sing Broadway tunes, Big Ten fight songs, and anything Irish. It didn't matter what it was, we just liked singing. I had thousands of half-remembered songs roaming around in my head that I was sure would keep me occupied until I reached Parga. I resumed the march with songs about states, starting with Ohio, of course.

I decided to throw my caution to the wet wind and hitchhike. There had only been an occasional car since I started walking, so my chances at getting a ride were slim. It was Easter Sunday, after all. Even the atheists were sitting around eating goat and breaking red eggs. As I stuck my thumb out, I thought about my father, who forbade his girls to ever hitchhike. It was okay for his boys to do it, in the same way it was okay for them to work when they were in high school. I thought it unfair on both accounts. No cars were in sight. Maybe my father was praying that I wouldn't get a ride just to teach me a lesson? The only thing to do was to counter with a prayer of my own. I said, sincerely, "Dear guardian angel, please, please send a car my way." She worked fast. With the "amen" still on my lips, I heard and then saw a car slow down and pull over. I waddled over. "Parga?" I sniffled into the window at the smiling, well-dressed and dry couple inside. They responded in English, "Sure, it's not out of our way. Get in." Gratefully, I put my soggy self in the backseat and thanked my angels, those above and in the front seat, for this dry car. In the midst of our conversation it came out that the driver was the coach of the Greek Olympic swimming team. I knew that when I wrote my mother about him she would be rooting for the Greek swimming team in the Olympics against anyone, except the US, of course, in thanks for him helping her daughter.

It took less than an hour to reach Parga. The couple dropped me off at the end of Brigit's street. When I walked in the door she took one look at me and helped me out of my wet clothes and into her fluffy, terry cloth robe. I stared to cry as I told her my saga of betrayal by my hero and the long walk on the empty road. "Men!" was all she answered as she sat me down at the blue table and bent my towel-covered head over a steaming pot filled with water, eucalyptus and pine. I breathed it in deeply as she packed my clothes, books and journal into my mismatched suitcases. She offered to swap my white summer blouse for a warm sweater that she thought I'd need for the trip. I don't think she actually wanted my old blouse; this was just her motherly way of making sure I had something warm to wear. I definitely got the best of the swap—that black sweater saw me through all the future winters I would spend in Europe. I felt bad that I couldn't properly clean my little room or do something special for her before I left, but Brigit was pretty matter-of-fact about what a stupid thing that was to worry about at this point. We had supper and then she sent me off to bed because the German guys would be leaving at six thirty in the morning…on the dot.

Omega: Home

I spent most of the road trip south curled up in the backseat, trying to keep my germs to myself. The boys did their part by not turning their heads in my direction when they addressed the odd word my way. I didn't stir from my cocoon until we arrived at the ferry that would take us across the Bay of Corinth to Patras and the Peloponnese, where, I knew from my struggle through Homer's *Odyssey,* a lot of important people had hung out.

I'm a big fan of ferries and have stood at the railing of every ferry I'd ever been on to watch the departure from one shore and the arrival at a new one. I wasn't going to miss this one, even if it turned out to be my trip across the River Styx. The boys told me I was crazy as they ordered beers and chips for themselves and a hot tea with a slurp of brandy in it for me. I bundled up as best I could and pushed open the door against a pretty serious spring-chilled wind. Staggering to the railing, I held on to keep from falling with the crash of the gray waves against the boat. Maybe the boys were right. But then the boat started chugging out of the harbor and I inched my way to the front to watch the arrival on the other shore. When we finally pulled into Patras, sitting on the very tip of the Peloponnese, my cold seemed to have disappeared somewhere within my frozen body. Fresh sea air was indeed the cure. While standing out there, I had made the decision to leave the boys and head for "home" in Loutraki over by Corinth—the opposite direction the boys were taking. They seemed disappointed, probably because it was one less person to share the cost of gas, but maybe just because they liked having me around. I was a little sad about missing the trip to Olympia—home of the gods and athlete's foot—but I would get there later.

Loutraki, according to my tour book, was famous for its water, touted as being equal to the nectar of the gods to restore health and wellbeing. I expected one of those musty-smelling spa towns I had seen in the Black Forest. What I found was a resort with fancy-looking hotels, restaurants, gift shops and cafés. It didn't look like any of the other places I had come to call home during this trip. Had I made a mistake? I walked into an empty café, where a bored-looking, white-jacketed waiter came to take my order. His plastic name tag, stamped in all caps, told me he was ADONIS. He was short and had what looked like either the start of a beard or leftovers from a sloppy shaving job on his face—this did not fit with his name, at least not in my book. As I stared, he waited. I wanted to go right into my spiel about needing a room with a place to cook but I hesitated, not wanting to be one of those Americans who just assumed everyone spoke English and barreled in with their demands without a care for the protocol of the culture. I ordered a coffee instead.

When he returned, he asked, in English, where I was staying. Am I just particularly blessed with bumping into these semi-gods of wayfarers? That little bit of kindness set me off on a retelling of my convoluted journey from Brindisi through Igoumenitsa and Parga. I told him all about Easter, my cold, hitching a ride with the swimming coach, the generous German boys and finally arriving at his café in my search for a home. It must have been too much information, because he just shook his head and left without a word. As I sat there, wondering how long I could nurse the tiny cup of coffee and discreetly counting my drachmas to see if I had enough to stay in one of those hotels for the night, Adonis returned. He had shed the white jacket and name tag and was wearing a faded black suit coat the color of his beard. He motioned for me to stand up and I obliged, since he had picked up my luggage and was headed out the door. He turned left, then left again past the faucet where you could fill your jugs with that miraculous water for free, and headed down a road that skirted the bay until we were out of the tourist Loutraki and into the land where the real people lived. We climbed past tiny white houses tucked here and there among glorious-smelling pines, small shops and neighborhood-size bars and ended up at a dead-end enclave of houses. Adonis dropped the suitcases and went into the biggest of the two houses.

In true Greek myth manner, I believe that my weeks of moving here and there with dirty sheets and pneumonia had all been necessary. My struggles were rewarded with this sunny patio with flowers and grape arbor and little benches planted under trees for contemplation. Then the door opened and Adonis came out with his mother, Kyrie Hermione. I wanted to start singing, "Kyrie, *eleison*," the only Greek I had learned during my Latin mass days, but knew it was always important to make a good first impression on the landlady, so I kept quiet. At that first meeting, I pegged Hermione to be in her late fifties or early sixties, mostly from her curly gray hair and her badge of widowhood—the ubiquitous black housecoat. (I now realize that she was probably in her late forties. I was seeing her through that leftover, smug, twenty-something arrogance which had us negating anyone over the age of thirty.) As Adonis faced his mother and started talking, I assumed he was telling her about my need for a place with sheets, towels and a kitchen stove, but he must have thrown in something more because Kyrie smiled sincerely and gave me a hug.

I could have cried. It had been so long since someone had done that on the first day. Hermione linked her arm in mine and led me to the stairs at the end of the garden. She unlocked a large, square room with a single window showing a sliver of the Bay of Corinth through the pine trees. This would be mine until June, when her regular water-drinker residents would come to spend their month in this paradise. The bathroom was outside and off the terrace but, with its proper plumbing, it couldn't be called an outhouse. Adonis came in with sheets and towels and Hermione and I made the bed. Then they left me to get settled.

It took me about ten minutes to settle in, since ninety percent of my clothes were dirty. Unpacking at that point was just a matter of taking the plastic bag out of my suitcase and putting it into the closet. I arranged my precious last two unread English books on a tiny shelf over the dresser and hoped they'd miraculously multiply during the night. I tucked my journal and pen on the bedside table where they waited for me to be inspired. There it was, home sparse home.

The first few days in a new house, no matter how welcome, is always a shy and slightly awkward time for me. I wasn't like the water drinkers—they had a real reason to be here. How could I explain that I was just looking for home, especially since I didn't really understand that myself? There were also the huge initial barriers of language and culture, which kept me sitting on my bed. Hermione must have sensed my uneasiness because she called me from the garden. She might have been quoting Socrates, but I chose to translate it as "Ana, come and see the kitchen." It's amazing how much you can understand of a language if you just stop worrying about looking like a fool. Hermione made some syrupy-sweet Greek coffee, which tasted much like the coffee I had in Dubrovnik. Then she gave me the tour of the kitchen. She showed me how to light the stove and where to put the garbage. When she finished I went out in search of food.

I remembered seeing a small grocery store on the way up the hill, so I set off in that direction. I made a mental shopping list and it sounded a lot like my initial shopping lists in all the other countries I'd lived in. My small food budget meant that I ate a lot of starches, dried beans, very little meat and only vegetables that were in season. This meager diet had turned me into a food voyeur—hungrily peeking into restaurant windows and standing outside bakeries just to smell the pastries. In retrospect, my decision to be frugal with my groceries was an unfortunate one, since I missed out on so much of the goodness that each country and culture offered. (I took my spending entirely too seriously. I still have the list I kept during my travels that shows the cost of each food item in every country I visited: Jam: Yugoslavia 8.60 dinars; Italy 500 lira; France 2.85 francs; Spain 25 pesetas, etc.)

The shop was tiny and crowded and, somehow, I instinctively knew the protocol—wait outside until one of the other women left. When I finally made my way inside I tripped over a beautiful little girl and squatted down to say hello. The baby was immediately whisked upward past my nose and into the arms of her mother. I looked up at her from my kneeling position and said, smiling, "Beautiful," pointing to the baby. I then heard a clucking sound—Ptooe!—all around me as each of the other women in the shop surrounded the baby and spat on her—at least, that's what it looked like to me. They gave me a slit-eyed stare that I had no trouble translating as "get the hell out of here." But I was hungry and this was the only store I'd seen on our climb, so I waited my turn. There was no chit-chat, no friendly smile as I bought my pasta, canned tomatoes, olive oil, soap powder and yogurt. I knew I'd have to find a different place to buy my food. When I told Adonis about this he said I had better get myself an evil eye fast, because those women thought I'd put a spell on that baby and they might do the same to me. I stopped in a tiny jewelry shop on the corner, bought one and looped it next to my miraculous medal and guardian angel on the chain around my neck. It must have worked, because I had no warts growing on my nose or unexplained accidents while I was in Greece.

One day Hermione decided that it was time for me to learn to cook like a Greek. We began with dolmades, since the grape leaves were perfect on her brother's vines. I have always been genuinely enthusiastic and thankful when these women would take me into their kitchens to teach me. I think my sincerity touched and flattered them. Even Frau Sofia softened when she showed me how to make *Grah*, her bean and potato dish. Hermione called me into the garden to hold the ladder while she climbed up on the roof of her brother's house. She was amazingly flexible for the sixty-year-old I thought she was as she crawled on all fours across the roof to get the spring-green leaves. She said she wouldn't take too many from one place because he'd know she'd been here. In the kitchen we washed, de-stemmed, then steamed the leaves. And as I watched, perched on a stool next to the stove, she put glugs of olive oil in a skillet followed by handfuls of chopped onions and parsley, a tea cup of rice, one big dollop of tomato paste and a wine glass of water. I tried to translate it all into more familiar measurements for future reference—cups, tablespoons, teaspoons—but it was impossible. She cooked it all together and then let it cool while we drank coffee. Then came my biggest challenge: rolling the dolmades. It looked easy enough when she did it. I followed her lead and put a leaf in the palm of my hand, tucked a teaspoon of rice in the middle and rolled. It fell apart; Hermione laughed. I tried again, she laughed again. By the tenth attempt I was getting frustrated but not hopeless. Then it happened: without trying, I had it. My teacher clapped her approval and sat down to let me practice on the ten or so that were left. I added mine to the already half-full pan of Hermione's perfectly wrapped leaves. When I finished, she poured a generous amount of olive oil and just enough water to cover them. They steamed while we watched a Greek soap opera that I could understand from the tone of voices, wrinkles of brows and my in-depth research into romance novels. When the dolmades were finished to her liking, Hermione delicately took them out of the pot. She added a beaten egg yolk and lemon juice to the sauce in the pan and then dribbled it over the cooked leaves. She poured each of us a glass of red wine and we sat around her kitchen table as I tasted my first dolmades, made with my own hands, no less. Every time I've made dolmades since then I give homage to Hermione for her patience and care in teaching me well.

My days were sweet during that last month before the water drinkers descended their unhealthy bodies upon Loutraki. The spring sun made the days warm enough to sit on the beach and wade in the still-chilly Bay of Corinth. I was usually the only person on the beach, since the Greeks were too busy sweeping out winter's dust, getting ready to make summer's money. One day, as I splashed my toes and thought about all the other toes that had walked upon this rocky beach, I looked up and saw that a young woman had parked herself right next to my tiny towel on the beach. I looked around and confirmed that there was not another person on that beach and felt a bit put out that she had plopped down right next to me. But what really startled me was that she was holding in her hands my half-read Dos Passos's *U.S.A Trilogy*. My books were rare treasures to me and to think that this woman may just walk away with one of them got me moving fast as I could across those pebbles. As it turned out, her name was Marina and she was from Detroit. She had been starved for English conversation with anyone other than her dour husband (I hadn't met him yet but when I did, the adjective fit), her two-year-old and her old Greek relatives in the mountains. Since she was a Midwesterner like me, I let her talk.

Unlike most young mothers, Marina's tale did not revolve around her child. Rather, with an animated voice and fervent hand gestures, she told me her story of being a free, wild girl just two years earlier in a Detroit high school. "It was far out," she said. She did things that no good Greek girl should ever have even known about. Every morning, to the protest of her mother, she would iron her thick, black hair so it would be as straight as Cher's, and then, with mother out of the room, she'd wiggle her way into the tightest jeans that could possibly make their way over her thighs. "I had to lie on the bed to get the zip up," she remarked proudly. I was envious. I had been raised in a family where girls did not wear short-shorts or tight jeans. (I remember when my older brother brought his sweetheart home to meet the family, she told us little sisters that she would put her shorts into the dryer to get them as tight and short as possible. It was scandalously delicious to hear her stories.)

Marina's tale soon became more of a lament as she, with her head hung in shame, told of one drunken night with a boy from her school. He was no one special, just some boring guy, but that night with him had been her one and only slip below that invisible line that we girls drew when it came to necking. And, just like the propaganda preached, it only took once to get pregnant. As a good Greek girl of the 1970s, she married the guy and waited for the baby. She was only nineteen and already felt her life was over. It was a worthy tale to be told on this Greek shore. All it needed was a chorus of Greek women to wail over the plight of poor Marina, but she only had me to give her my "Ohs".

After the telling there was nothing to be done but walk the beach arm-in-arm, exchange addresses and promise that we'd keep in touch. Before she left Marina gave me a gift that far exceeded the mere listening I'd done for her—she showed me where the books were hidden. Among the dozen or so hotels that lined the beach were three where the English water drinkers stayed. In those lobbies, open for all to see, were tables of English-language books. "All you have to do is walk in like you belong there." If you leave a book you can take a book, or sometimes even two if no one is watching. Durell's *Alexandria Quartet* would be my first trade, entitling me to four new books. I was exhilarated by the adventure of sneaking into the hotel, but even more so by the suspense of what I would find on that table. That summer I read biographies of people I had never even heard of, held my breath with le Carré and sunk myself into romances. I became totally addicted to those saucy, shirt-ripping, hot tales of lust that vacationers seemed to favor. These stories supplied a certain sexual stimulation without the emotional quagmire I always got myself into with real men. They were wonderful.

Hermione's water drinkers came and went throughout the summer, except for Monsieur Jean, who was staying in my square room at the top of the stairs. He was a Greek man who now lived in Paris, France. He came early in June and left at the beginning of September. He told me he'd been coming to drink the water and flirt with Hermione every summer for the past twenty years. Since he and I were the regulars from week to week, we enjoyed a more privileged position in the house, which included an afternoon coffee under the trees with Hermione. Most days Monsieur Jean (when he wasn't down drinking the water) would sit under the apricot tree reading philosophy. While I crawled around his feet picking up fallen apricots for jam, he would drop words of wisdom down onto my bent head. I can't remember what I learned back then, but I do remember feeling uplifted mentally from my crawling position. I always gave him a small jar of jam as my tuition.

Throughout the summer I made little excursions to visit in person some of the places that I had read about. The longest trip I made was to Delphi to confer with the oracle about my future. For someone who believes in angels and saints, it wasn't hard to extend that belief to oracles—but she only spoke in riddles and I was always lousy at getting those. I did not become a water drinker that summer since I didn't like the musty smell of the spa where the genuine water drinkers hung out. What I did become was a water splasher. Almost every day I'd walk down to the beach and wade into the water up to my neck with all the other women and children who didn't know how to swim. I'd look enviously out to the open space where the deep water started and the swimmers didn't have to deal with the screams and cries of spoiled children. I had never lived around water long enough to learn how to swim. When I was in high school the first pool in our neighborhood opened up, but it was too expensive for our family to get a membership. I felt I was destined to become a wader and splasher for all the days of my water life. It seemed a pity here in this beautiful, warm, ancient sea.

One day while I was walking on the beach I found a pair of flippers. They were someone's rejects, left on the edge of the beach like someone had walked out of them from the sea and didn't even think they were worth an additional trip to the trash bin. They weren't pretty, that's for sure; the flipper part had been reconnected to the foot part by bits of unmatched wire that looked like they had been bent out of coat hangers. I didn't care. They were my ticket to get beyond the shallows. The next day I walked down to the beach and spent time watching other flipper-clad swimmers get into the water. There was a certain skill to maneuvering these rubber clown feet. I took at least three full-frontal flips into the waves before I was on my back, cruising with amazing speed away from the splashers and waders and into the open water. Before long the splashers' screams had quieted and the hotels were shrunken. I started to feel a panic coming on, but a twitch of my flipper kept me afloat and sailing back toward the shore. I was liberated. No longer was I tied to the shallow waters at the beach. With flippers in tow, I could slip into the water at any of the little coves that dotted the coast around Loutraki. I felt reckless and confident, but not so much that I stopped praying that the wire would hold as I swam farther and farther from shore.

By mid-July all of the tenants in Hermione's rooms were friends and relatives. Her brother, Theodore, had come from Athens with his wife and assorted members of the family. All the other rooms were occupied by people who had been coming for years. Monsieur Jean knew everyone's stories, which he told me during our time under the apricot tree. Hermione started bringing the television out to the garden at night and all of us would carry out a chair so we could watch whatever she turned on. I loved this, because the Greeks wisely did not dub English programs but used subtitles. It gave me an inside track to punch lines. Every Thursday we watched *Thriller*, a British suspense show and Hermione's favorite. If I wasn't outside when it was about to start, she would come to my screen door and say, "Ana, Twiller!" One Thursday night *Thriller* was all about a woman being stalked by this man she knew was going to murder her. She conveniently had a detective boyfriend who said not to worry, honey. I knew that he was useless and so did she and everyone else on the patio after they'd read the subtitles. This woman worked in a big office building and always had to work late. One night she knew the guy was in the building and called boyfriend, who says not to worry again, they have him trapped, and sends her home ALONE in her little mini. I'm screaming at the television, "Don't go, don't go," and by that time everyone else had read the subtitles and they were shouting at her too not to be so stupid. The murderer, of course, is in the backseat of her car when she gets in. She kills him with her nail file or something. Hermione was enthralled and squealed her approval. I thought about the episode every time I had to work overtime alone in that big law firm in Washington. Sometimes the lights would go off as the guard made his rounds, forgetting that I was there...or was it the guard?

Hermione and I shared the big kitchen in the house as the outside one got too busy with all the regulars. I think she figured I'd be less of a bother, since I wouldn't be spending cooking time chit-chatting about other things. By that time we were good friends in our language-challenged relationship. She continued to teach me how to cook her dishes and I taught her English phrases, which she accented with a huge laugh every time she said them. That summer she showed me how to take fillets of thick white fish and set them on a bed of fresh, chunky slices of tomatoes with onions, garlic, parsley and oregano. She would simmer it all on top of the stove until the fish easily broke apart. She would also cook tiny meatballs spiced up with mint and oregano from the pots by the door. Sometimes she didn't bother with a lesson but just sat me down at the table and put food in front of me. I think secretly she missed having a daughter, so I had become a thankful fill-in, if only for a few months.

When the Montreal Olympics started we'd all spend every night from ten p.m. to one a.m. watching them. It was too hot to be inside, even in my screen-windowed room, so having something to watch on television that late in the night was a gift from the gods and Hermione. My mother wrote that it was remarkable to her that she and I were watching the same Olympics at the same time in such different parts of the world. By the beginning of September the water drinkers began to filter out. As if the weather knew this, it got blustery and cloudy on days that just a week before had been hot and clear. Monsieur Jean was the last to leave; he drove into Athens with Theodore to catch his train to Paris. He told me he never flew because the transition from paradise to city would be too dramatic. I remember thinking that his words were a bit extreme. I mean, he did live in Paris, after all.

Hermione invited me to move back into the big square room at the top of the stairs and stay for the winter. She wanted me to make it my home. But before I could say yes, I knew that I had to make a convincing case with the Tourist Police to persuade them to extend my visa and let me stay in Greece. I had been here just about a week shy of my six-month visa expiring. I am always intimidated by police, no matter what the country, especially those who had such power that for any offending detail—maybe the color of my hair—they could boot me out of their country, never to return again. That was what it felt like when the Tourist Police denied my application to stay, although they did give me the grace of an extra month to plan my exit. They didn't give me a reason, so maybe it was my hair color. I suspected at the time that they probably already had their quota of twenty-something Americans in the country and just didn't want any more clogging up their beaches and healthcare system.

The next day, as if the message was delivered by the winged-foot Hermes himself, I received a letter from an acquaintance in Washington who knew of my traveling and offered me the use of his time share on the Mediterranean Coast of Spain in exchange for giving it a thorough cleaning while I was there. My next destination had been determined by forces far beyond me, or so it seemed. There was nothing to be done but to pack my two suitcases, take books to the hotels to exchange for new ones to get me through the journey and beyond, and, finally, throw out my wired flippers.

Hermione called Theodore to tell him I had to leave, and he helped me to find and book passage on a Turkish freighter leaving Piraeus on the Aegean, and then on to the Mediterranean to Barcelona with stops in Naples and Marseille along the way. To save money I booked steerage, which gave me a hammock in the girls' dormitory, shared showers and nothing else. When Hermione found out I'd have to bring my own food, she fixed enough parcels of non-perishable foods to get me as far as Naples. When it was time to take the bus to Athens, she and Adonis walked with me on the same path that had led me to their house those six months before. It seemed to me as I rode the bus into Athens that the gods must surely be telling me that this Odyssey of mine wasn't over yet—I still had to find home.

Finding Home

Benidoleig, Spain
1976

There was something comforting about holding a map with an "X" marking the exact location of my next home. Well, not really home, since I could only stay there for two weeks. It was more the comfort of finding a temporary resting place, like seeing the orange roof of a Howard Johnson motel after a long day of driving. And there were those strings of cleaning the place and closing it down for the winter attached to my free rent. But even that seemed inviting, especially after braving a rough Mediterranean Sea in an even rougher Turkish freighter to get here.

It all seemed fine when I boarded the boat in Piraeus, headed for Barcelona. The Turkish boat company offered steerage passage to anyone willing to pack her own food, drink Nescafé made with hot water from the tap in the bathroom sink and sleep in a hammock in a below-deck dormitory. There were separate rooms with the words "girls" and "boys" printed on the door in three different languages, just to make sure we understood the rules. The Turkish captain evidently did not want any hanky-panky going on below decks. But he did not appreciate the resourcefulness of sexually hungry twenty-somethings in the era of Free Love. Within hours of leaving Piraeus, the one shower stall with a lock was commandeered as the rendezvous place, the line formed to the left. I never visited it except to take a shower at the odd times it wasn't otherwise occupied. I had always wanted a shipboard romance, but not that kind. You wouldn't have found Bette Davis in *Now Voyager* agreeing to meet Paul Henreid in the below-deck shower room. They had style, and anyway, they were traveling first class. That's the romance I dreamed about—some "him" lighting two cigarettes at the same time while looking longingly into my eyes through the smoke as the moon rippled on the sea beyond. It didn't happen. I lit my own cigarettes and never wrote to my mother about the shower room.

That boat, a train and two buses brought me to the spot marked with the "X." It was a seaside resort on the Costa Blanca called Nova Denia, halfway between Alicante and Valencia. It did not look like the picture I had in my head from Wayne's letter. He had described this place as "happening," but the only thing happening here today was a rain-threatening wind blowing sea mist through the tree-tall oleanders (I found out much later that that's what they were called) and into my eyes. There wasn't one single person outside, but really, it was a Thursday at the end of October, and who would go to a seaside resort in the off season except for me. But this wasn't like going to Loutraki or Amalfi in the off season; there, real people lived, and those places had butchers and greengrocers and bars. Here there was nothing but a row of very nice-looking-on-the-outside abandoned villas with a see-you-next-year look about them. Was it really worth the saved rent to spend two weeks by myself with no one around within screaming distance?

Unfortunately, I took that minute to remember my experience at a similarly abandoned seaside resort on Isla Mujeres in Mexico, where I had accidentally kicked the resident dog on my way back from the showers (it was dark, the dog was black, I was innocent). The growling bark from Fido brought his owner out of his office with machete in hand. He shouted at me to be careful around his dog and, to emphasize his warning, swiped his machete on an unfortunate bush. Needless to say, I didn't sleep much that night.

Wayne's instructions were very clear: look for *número* 24, where I would find Señor Miguel Fornes, who held the key to the "X" on my map. (I quietly prayed he did not own a machete.) Anyone who has spent any time in a Mediterranean country knows that you never arrive between one and five in the afternoon and expect to be welcomed. I knew this well, but I was the captive of a bus service that didn't think it was all that important to run buses in October after one thirty in the afternoon to this seaside resort. I had no choice but to arrive here when everyone else was home eating and sleeping. So I wasn't surprised when nothing but silence answered my knock on the door. Señor Fornes was probably in a bar somewhere playing dominoes and wouldn't be back for a couple of hours. I was tempted to park my two suitcases and backpack on his porch and head down the road to the sea, but since I wasn't sure about the neighborhood and who might still be lurking behind these dark windows, I plunked myself down on his porch step and pulled a book at random from the supply I'd gotten from the hotel in Loutraki. (I was still feeling guilty that I had taken more books than what I had left on the table. Mea culpa.)

Fifty pages into the steamy story about Mrs. Simpson and King Edward, he arrived. Señor Fornes was remarkably short, even for a Spaniard, and very dapperly dressed for a Thursday, midday. I started to suspect that he had been stacking something other than dominoes during his siesta. He smiled and gallantly picked up one of my suitcases (the lightest one) and led me down the sand-packed street to the opposite end to *número* 24. While the house we stopped at did have the advantage of being next to the sea, I was a little apprehensive of being down here all by myself. Señor Fornes started backing off the porch as soon as he handed me the key. At the bottom of the steps he called back to me to say he'd pick me up tomorrow at nine a.m. to take me into Denia to do some shopping. I must have looked surprised, because he started to explain that the bus didn't run every day and he was sure I would need "*cosas.*" I thought it was strange and very un-Spanish that he didn't come in to show me around the place, get me settled and then invite me back to his house for a *copa* of wine or coffee or something. But as soon as I opened the door I understood why Señor Fornes did not come in with me. The place made Miss Havisham's dining room look like a spread for *Better Homes and Gardens.* It looked like Wayne and his friends had just picked up and left as soon as their last supper was consumed—a week or so ago. I could practically write a script on that party just from counting the number of empty beer, wine and gin bottles and the full ashtrays. The whole mess made me question the wisdom of taking Wayne's dangling carrot of free rent. I would have cried and left but there was no way for me to get back to Denia, where there would be comforts like clean hotels and restaurants. So all I could do was survey the territory and hope that there were some clean towels and sheets somewhere in the house.

As disheartening as the tour of the full sink, overflowing garbage and sticky floor in the kitchen was, there were some positive finds—a few recognizable vegetables in the refrigerator, an unopened box of pasta, a bottle of olive oil and, best of all, three bottles of red wine, corks in. I would at least be able to eat and drink if not be merry. I decided the best I could do to survive the night was to stack everything in neat little piles, fix my dinner and retreat back to the one clean bedroom with the scandalous story of the abdicating king and his divorced lover and a bottle of wine. Before I went to sleep I whispered a short, hopefully effective prayer to St. Anthony, patron saint of all animals: "Please, Tony, if your friends the rats have discovered this place, ask them to move on before the morning. Thank you and Amen."

The mess didn't look any better in the morning. I sat down, coffee-less, and made a list of what I would need. I'm sure that these were what Señor Fornes was referring to as "*cosas.*" (I fleetingly thought of sending Wayne a bill for the supplies, but knew I couldn't.) I added enough food items to get me through to Monday, when the bus would run again to get me into town for more shopping. Señor Fornes was prompt for a Spaniard. On the drive into Denia I attempted a bit of conversation, pulling out of my memory the Spanish I had learned in Seville. I knew I had failed when he switched to his own unique version of English halfway there.

Denia is a sweet little town, nestled under its own castle next to the sea with a beautiful, tree-canopied street running through its center. Señor Fornes parked himself in a café there and directed me to certain shops, which I'm sure were all owned by his friends. I was thankful I had had those seven months in Seville to learn the basics of "How to Shop in Spain": wait my turn; just accept graciously that things were kept behind the counter out of reach, putting the onus on me to find the word, gesture at the clerk or employ telepathic powers to tell her what I wanted; and that I should smile a lot to cover any American faux pas I was sure to make. When I went into the hardware/dry goods store, a very proper, tall man wearing a blue cotton jacket over his shirt bowed to me and waited. I smiled, then pointed at a mop and a bucket. He took the lead on cleaners, pulling scouring powder, ammonia, dish soap, cloths and garbage bags off the shelf. I wanted to applaud and kiss him for anticipating me before I had to go through my pantomime. He wrapped each purchase in a slice of white wrapping paper kept on a big roll on the counter, placed them all gently into my bag and then walked with me to the door, opened it and bowed me out. It was the most elegant experience I had ever had buying household cleaners.

There was a part of me that was excited about the challenge of attacking this Herculean-sized cleaning job. I was, after all, well qualified; I had grown up with six brothers who would stay up late watching TV and leave full ashtrays, empty chip bags and an assortment of bottles for their sisters to clear the next morning. Even then, at age twelve, I took a certain pleasure in making order out of their mess (until they did it again the next night and then I'd just get angry). It took five changes of water, half a bottle of dish soap and one pair of very red hands to get all the dishes washed, the counters wiped down and the floor mopped. When that was done, I sat down at the table with a glass of wine and a cigarette to admire my work. After two days of cleaning it was done, and I decided that the next day, Sunday, I would explore the beach to see if I could find a place to celebrate my little victory over grunge. Well, okay, it was also because I knew I was all alone on the street. Señor Fornes had stopped by to say he would be leaving and wouldn't be back until Monday morning, when he'd be happy to take me into Denia to the *mercado*. I figured he spent the weekend at his mother's house or had a secret family locked away in Denia. Even before he left the porch I started to feel that creepy kind of lonely that I get when I know I am absolutely the only person alive on my planet, or at least my street. Tomorrow I would head off on my own to find others.

When You Least Expect It...

One thing I knew for certain about Spanish culture was that, if there were more than two Spaniards living someplace, there had to be a bar within walking distance. Even though my street was abandoned, that didn't mean there weren't some real people living out this way who would be eating tapas and having a *copa* this Sunday afternoon. So, keeping the Spanish clock in mind, I set off from the house at one o'clock, knowing that if any place was going to be open, it would be open then. My oasis appeared after twenty minutes of walking along the beach, fighting strong winds, wet sand and a splashing ocean. There, on a little gravel side road nestled among some pine trees, was a one-story pink building with a front porch held up by four white peeling pillars at each corner. From inside came the lovely, welcoming sound of clinking glasses and loud voices, assuring me that yes, indeed, they were open. I had found my local.

On Sunday everyone, even the women, came out for a drink. So I should have been ready for that silent, head-to-toe scrutiny that every woman in the place gave me when I walked in. I had been getting a similar once-over in every country I had visited since I left home, but they thankfully lost interest in me almost instantly. I chose a table in the corner and took out Edward and Wallis and my pack of Celtas for company. I loved smoking Celtas and that jaunty horned Viking on the pack. Ever since I left Seville I had missed their black-tobacco smelly taste—having them back again was like reuniting with an old friend after a separation. (Later, one of my friends in the village would say to me, "Ana, you smoke the cigarettes of the Communists," and slap me on the back in a "we're-in-this-together" kind of way. I didn't tell him that I had initially bought them because they were the cheapest brand available, but then maybe that's what made them the cigarettes of the people. Much later, after he and I had gotten to know each other better, he drunkenly explained to me one night what he really meant: "CELTAS: *Comunistas Españoles, Levantaos, Tenéis Ayuda Soviética!*" which I roughly translated as "Yo, Spanish Communists, rise up and help the Soviets." I never told my mother I was smoking Communist cigarettes; she would have been silently disappointed in me.) I ordered *una caña* and *tortilla*. The waiter rolled his eyes, sensing my frugality, or maybe it was my Celtas that gave my penny-pinching away. But he brought my small beer and piece of omelet just the same, with that graceful but slightly resentful way that Spanish waiters had, especially with single women. In spite of their poor manners, I was always falling secretly in love with them.

I settled in to spend the day there, but by three all the families had moved on to their dining-room tables for lunch and only a couple of guys at the bar, the bartender and me were left. I knew from the look the waiter gave me when he brought my second beer that they really wanted to close up and go home for siesta. I was raised to always respect the worker and, after all, everyone is entitled to their siesta, so I drank the beer down faster than I wanted to, packed up my book, the Celtas, paper and pen, said *gracias* and *adios* and headed back down the beach to my clean house, feeling a whole lot less alone than I had when I walked out the door.

Next morning, Señor Fornes was at my door disconcertingly promptly at ten a.m. to take me to Denia's weekly street market. I didn't even try to use my Spanish with him, since he started the day with a "Good morning." When we got to Denia, instead of parking himself at the same café, he led me to Casa Pepe, a bar that overlooked the pretty little park that marked the center of the town. In my personal rulebook, noon was the absolute earliest that I could drink alcohol. Any time before that seemed a sure indication of my hidden alcoholism; I was convinced that if I had a drink now, at ten thirty a.m., before too long I would start hiding gin bottles under flower pots the way Lee Remick did in *Days of Wine and Roses*. Not so the patrons of Casa Pepe, who seemed to be well into a day of drinking. It appeared that everyone in this bar except for Señor Fornes and me was a Brit. Anytime I am so outnumbered, I keep my mouth shut. When the bartender asked me what I wanted (in English), I answered, "*Un café.*" I'm sure I didn't fool him for a minute, but I had endured too many insults from Brits about how my nasal Midwestern accent brutalized the English language. I didn't feel like laying myself open to a whole bar of jokes. Señor Fornes wasn't helping, since he insisted on talking to me in English. I would answer him either with silence or a few whispered words. He looked at me strangely. Then, just when I thought I'd have to leave before he gave me away, from the back of the bar where the pool tables lived I heard a loud, definitely American, female voice say, "Jack, get your ass back over here right now. I mean it." That was my introduction to Doris McClowsky and her brood of five boys.

When I saw the size of Doris I wondered how anyone could possibly not do what she said. She was enormous, not fat but very tall and broad shouldered, with hands twice the size of mine. Doris was just a big, big woman. In fact, she sort of resembled that Viking on my Celtas package, minus the horned cap. Señor Fornes waved her over to join us. It seemed that the two of them were old friends, because she bent down and kissed him on both cheeks. She sent Jack and his brothers outside to work off boy energy and then, over another coffee for me and a beer for her, I found out that Doris, from Milwaukee, had come to Spain a few months earlier to get away from "everything" after her lucrative divorce from a brewery executive. Since she had started life out as a farm girl, she thought it was time to return to the soil, just not Wisconsin soil, so she bought a farmhouse in the middle of an orchard. At this, she smiled at Señor Fornes, and he at her. (Could he have gone to Doris's for the weekend? The thought of the two of them as lovers conjured up some shocking lovemaking pictures in my mind.) Doris said she was fixing the place up herself. She reasoned that hard labor would help her get over her broken heart or anger, whichever sentiment she felt at the first blow of a hammer. I liked this woman, and not just because she was an American in a sea of Brits, really.

We skipped the market entirely and sat there long enough that eventually it was noon and I could order a beer. Over little plates of olives and salted almonds, Señor Fornes said, "Call me Miguel, *por favor*." He told me he was a real estate agent catering to the English-speaking trade. He had sold Doris her farm and had recruited her to get new clients. I figured she could just physically pick them up and plunk them down at his table for Monday morning meetings. Was she getting a commission or was she doing it for love? Doris decided that I was the obvious next client for his talents. I should have told her right then that I was not a good candidate for real estate. I had never owned anything substantial in my life—not a car or a house, not even a big dog. I remember getting a lecture from an accountant once who told me it was un-American not to have debt or a mortgage. I was really quite satisfied with being able to fit everything I owned in the world into two suitcases and a backpack, even though at the same time there was that part of me that always wanted a home and roots and a garden. But the idea of actually signing on the dotted line for a house was scarier to me than that machete-yielding Mexican. I tried to convince them of this, but Miguel and Doris were not dissuaded. By the third beer and a plate of fried squid (they were paying), I succumbed to their pressure and said sure, why not, it wouldn't cost me anything to look and it would get me off my empty street and out to places where people with cars could go. So, pretending to be a serious customer, I confessed to Miguel that I didn't have much money to spend, which only made him smile and Doris snort with laughter. I had nothing to lose if I just went with them and then, when my ten days at Wayne's were up, I'd tell Miguel and Doris that there was nothing I really liked and then I'd just say adios, go back to Washington as planned, get a job typing and milk my European memories for great party openers. But right now, they were both smiling at me and shaking my hand. That evidently made me an official client—and the search for home suddenly catapulted to the next level.

Shopping for a Spanish Caseta

I felt a little bad deceiving Miguel. He seemed so sincere about wanting to find me the perfect little Spanish *caseta*. I thought about calling the search off, but I was too late: we were already on the other side of Denia and there before me was *casa número uno*. It was a sweet little cottage with the sound of the sea just a breeze away. In my imagination I was already planting red geraniums out front and walking into town for coffee or beer. In the end, it wasn't the fact that I really wasn't interested in buying real estate that brought me back to reality; it was the huge, cone-dropping pine tree that towered above the house. It brought back a childhood memory of a house being crushed by a tree in the middle of a summer storm. All I could think of was that tree toppling on to me as I slept inside. Miguel said the price was three thousand U.S. dollars; I told him that was too expensive and never had to tell him about the tree.

He told me not to worry, there were others. We headed away from the sea (sigh) and into the valley, where tiny farming villages vied with orange trees for space. From what I could see, the trees were way ahead. When Miguel pulled off the road and into a small village where he had "connections," my gut started screaming, "Get out of this town and fast." I always trusted my gut when it came to finding a place to live. Mind you, if it had been close to the sea like Amalfi or Loutraki, I might have forgiven its flatness just a little, but it didn't even have a long-distance view of the sea. Flat, no sea view and a dirt-packed main street with blank-faced houses sitting smack dab on it so you'd have to look both ways just to leave your house. No, no, no. But it was too late to stop Miguel. He was already walking into the bar conveniently located right across from the church, so that worshippers didn't have to waste any time getting from God's table to Sunday tapas. I always respected the Spaniards' understanding of geography when it came to locating bars. When we walked in, one of the guys playing dominoes stood up and the three of us walked around the corner and down a dirt-paved street (how could this town get worse?) until we got to *casa número dos*—a very narrow two-story house. When we got inside, we had to walk single file back to where the only light bulb hung from the ceiling in the "sitting room." The owner pointed out the lovely fireplace, which Miguel assured me was in fine working order. I figured it would be impossible to light a fire in it given how close it was to the facing wall, which would probably catch fire from any heat it would throw off. It took us about twenty steps to walk from the front door to the back, where he proudly showed me the outhouse and the one sink with running water. I was not impressed until Miguel told me the asking price was one thousand dollars. You could buy a house in 1976 with running water and electricity and within a ten-minute drive to the Mediterranean for *one thousand dollars*? I was so wrapped up in the price of the place that I forgot I didn't even know how to drive, which would make it impossible to get there. My fantasy didn't last long because Miguel was telling the guy we'd get back to him later in the week. We were making no snap judgments, it seemed. By then it was getting dangerously close one p.m., and Miguel suggested that we leave *casa número tres* for mañana. I agreed because I knew that it is never a good idea to get between a Spaniard and his midday routine. We headed back to the church bar for beer and tapas.

Doris came with us the next day. I figured Miguel had asked her so that she could use her appeal as a fellow Midwesterner to reinforce his sales pitch. I was enjoying myself, sitting in the backseat trying to count the number of orange trees in a row and then estimating the number of oranges those trees would produce. (I would discover later that even though they called these *naranjas*, they weren't oranges but those tiny tangerines that come to us in the West in a wooden box to herald the onslaught of winter. Maybe in Spain they don't see any reason to differentiate one from the other; they're all citrus and they're all the same color, after all.) I had lost my count, but it didn't matter because I was pleased to see all those green leaves on trees this late in October.

This village was as hilly as yesterday's had been flat, and it was registering a positive high on my gut meter. The road going into town was straight up and ended at a little plaza in front of the church. Even if I had driven at the time, I don't think I would have done so in this town. Miguel had to pull over twice for cars coming the other way. When we got to the top of the hill Miguel shifted the car into the plaza and then the three of us walked down a narrow lane in between the whitewashed wall of the church and a row of four houses and a greengrocer. We stopped at one with a sign out front that read "*Vincente Ballester Ballester, Practicante.*" I didn't know what that meant, the Practicante part at least, but the sign looked official. A Miguel-sized, black-mustached, skinny man answered the door, shook hands all around and told us, "*Un momento, por favor.*" He closed the door in our faces and, as we waited, Doris filled me in on Señor Ballester Ballester. She said that he was the local shot-giver/prescription-writer but, more importantly, he was the Franco-appointed mayor of the town. I had forgotten about the Fascists. What was I doing even thinking of sticking around here? Memories bubbled up of the illegal strike in Seville and seeing those defenders of Fascism—the gun-toting, patent-leather-hatted Guardia Civil—on every street corner. My gut meter reading was certainly tempered by this news. When Señor B&B joined us I felt creepy walking up the hill with a real live Fascist. I wanted to tell everyone around me that I came from the land of freedom and liberty for all (well, sometimes, and usually then only for some people).

We started to climb. The hills in this town made for great vistas but brought up asthmatic complaints from my suffering, heaving, smoke-filled lungs. Maybe I'd give up my Celtas if I lived here. Probably not. Our destination was a house halfway to the top, where an elderly woman yielding a cane and wearing a black dress covered with a gray striped apron waited to join our little group. She took the lead, nodding and saying something to the women we passed on the way back down the hill we had just climbed. Most likely she was telling them she finally found someone foolish enough to buy her house. I just smiled at them and said *Hola.* We ended up on a dead-end street that was so steep we had to shuffle along with our knees bent and our bodies turned sideways, taking one small step at a time. All of us except the Señora, who placed her cane strategically in front of her and shuffled her slippered feet down that hill at an admirable clip. The location of the house was not a good sign, but the view was terrific. Spread out in front of me was the valley of those orange trees I had counted and real stone-faced mountains that I had missed from the car. My gut meter exploded a positive "YES" for *casa número tres.*

The Señora pulled a palm-sized key out of her apron pocket that opened a tiny door hidden inside a much bigger one. We all stepped into total darkness. I held onto Doris's shoulder because she was bigger than me and could, I was sure, protect me from whatever creatures were living there. Just when I started to contemplate backing out and into the view again, Miguel bent over and opened up the larger door, which let out a mournful creak. The light flooded in from outside and only confirmed my initial impression when I saw weeds growing out of the facade of the house. It seemed to me that this poor little house had been left on its own for far too long and, also, that real estate agents in Spain in the 1970s didn't require sellers to clean up even a little bit.

Sensing my hesitation to move forward into the darkness and actually beyond that darkness, Miguel, encouraged by Doris, went into real estate agent mode. The Señora stepped back and gave him the stage. Sure, it might resemble a barn right now, what with the straw all over the floor and, to my chagrin, a real machete on the wall (maybe I could use it as a hat rack), but it had been the Señora's husband's family home for more than five hundred years. Miguel explained that the Señora was forced to move out of her house by her sons, who worried about her being down here all alone. So, since the house was empty, she decided to help out her neighbor, Pedro, by letting him keep his rabbits here while he fattened them up for the butcher. This is a small town and everyone helps everyone else. But before the rabbits came, this had been the loving home of the Señora and her children. To make ends meet after her husband died—I knew I was getting sucked in now—the Señora took in sewing and her sons sold string to farmers and housewives who lived in the village. To illustrate the point, Miguel waved a hand at the ceiling to show me the big hook where the scale had hung and then, towards the foyer wall, on which all the additions and subtractions of their sales were scribbled. I had missed those in the darkness on the way in. I wanted to check to see if the additions were correct. But Miguel was on a roll and knew I was softening, especially when he talked about the family sitting by this lovely fireplace with its orange and cobalt-blue tiles reading their prayer books. I think the Señora understood some English, because she rolled her eyes at the last part. But, hey, I'm a sucker for stories about houses and the people (and animals?) who lived there. So I took the bait and moved deeper into the darkness.

Doris was whispering in my ear all the possibilities a piece of property like this had. Don't look at the dirt and the football-sized cobwebs, she said, picture it clean and furnished, with you sitting in front of that fire on a cold winter's night. It was hard for me to do that, since no amount of imagination could erase the outhouse at the back of the corral that we had stepped into when Miguel opened the big latch on the back door. I knew that never in this lifetime or the next would I be sitting over that hole. The thought of even going out there in the dark was enough to set me running for the light at the front of the house. I asked why they had a corral and the Señora stepped in and said proudly that they had had fifty goats at one time. There was no back gate, so I knew those goats had walked through the house every day, twice a day. When I peeked inside again I saw the goat-high black oily smear along the wall going from door-to-door and knew they probably left more than their lanolin on their daily trot. Doris caught a glance at my gaping mouth and propelled me out of the corral and up the stairs to the second floor, where more surprises lived.

There were actually two sets of stairs. I thought of that Robert Frost poem about taking the path less traveled, but both sets of stairs looked pretty worn so I just followed Doris's lead. Surprise number one came halfway up the stairs, where there was a room covered knee-deep in almond shells under the slant of the roof. I asked, "*Por qué?*" Miguel and Doris just shrugged, and the Señora had moved on up to open a shutter covering a tiny window that let in a bit of light to complement the pinpoints of sunshine I could see coming through the bamboo roof. Even I, having never been a homeowner before, knew that seeing daylight through your roof was not recommended by *Good Housekeeping*. But what interested me more right then were the super-sized tin can lids that were swinging from the rafters. Each lid was attached to a string like a Japanese lantern. But I sensed that there was nothing quite so festive about these particular hangings. The Señora proudly educated us to their use: when drying tomatoes for the winter, you secured them with string (probably the same product they sold downstairs) underneath the lids. She pointed with her cane so I'd understand. That way, she continued, when the rats climbed in through the bamboo roof, they would land on the top of the tin lids, lose their balance and, plunk, fall to the floor without a morsel of tomato to show for their effort. I wished she had never told me that. Rats and a machete. Were my nightmares following me here, and was it a sign that I absolutely should not be even remotely considering buying this house?

As I pondered this, the others had already started down the stairs. I hurried after them, just in case a mixed-up rat thought it was canning season. At the top of the other set of stairs, the Señora opened a flimsy wooden door and sunlight flooded in. The view that waited for me outside that door left me breathless. There before me was a 360-degree panorama of the mountains, the valley and the sea. I forgot the tin lids at once and let out a genuine "Ahh." With that, the Señora shook Miguel's hand and started down the stairs, leaving him to wrap up the final details of making me a homeowner. Doris put an arm around me like a friend, or a won commission.

Over beers at one of the three bars that sat facing the church (I wondered how all three could make a living in a small town like this), Miguel told me the asking price was twenty-two hundred but he was sure he could get it down to two thousand. Doris said I'd be crazy not to snatch it up. Even if I left it empty for another twenty-five years and leased it out for rabbit breeding, I'd still come out ahead. I had never in my life spent two thousand dollars on one thing. It made me nervous just thinking about it, but after some hesitation and a bit of internal argument, I decided to make my move. I agreed to go with Miguel to Señora's that evening to seal the deal, as they say. Doris was too busy to come. She had to knock down a wall or something or, I hoped, help the boys with their homework.

When we arrived at her home the Señora was sitting outside her door with knitting needles tucked under her arm still clicking away as she greeted us. I was always impressed how European women could carry on a conversation, watch kids and keep an eye on strangers' ascent up their hill without missing a stitch. It was then that she formally introduced herself to me as Señora Asunción Ballester Mas. My twelve years of indoctrination in Catholic schools had biased me, so I felt I had to trust anyone named after the Assumption of the Virgin Mary up into Heaven. However, she did have that Ballester in there, which meant she could have been related to the Fascist, and that made me uncomfortable about forming these kinds of business ties with her. But, really, it could be a different line of the family altogether. (I would find out later that there were not a lot of different family names in this village, which made me wonder about the mental health of future generations.) She grabbed her chair and led us into the house.

Señora Asunción introduced her three sons sitting at the table as Martine, the eldest, who lived in Denia where he worked in an office (she was obviously terribly proud of this achievement); Pepe, who had a good job working on the roads and still lived with Señora; and Efaristo, the skinniest and youngest of the three, who lived in Pedreguer down the road and worked as a janitor in the local school and occasionally as a leather cutter in one of the purse factories. His greatest claim to fame, according to Señora, was the fact that he and his wife had produced a child after twenty-five years of marriage when they were both well into their forties. They had been invited to this meeting to help Señora with translation and to meet the new owner of their family home.

Sealing the Deal

As we sat, Miguel went into negotiation mode, but Señora Asunción raised her hand and stopped him in mid-offer. She looked at me and through Miguel asked me point blank: did I want to buy her house, fix it up and then sell it to other foreigners, or was I planning to live there? She sat back while Miguel translated. I wondered if this was a trick question. I smiled—my mother had told me it always helps—and explained how I had been traveling for the past five years and longed for a little place of my own, where I could unpack my two suitcases and be there for longer than three months and maybe even plant a garden (but not in the facade of my house). I smiled again to show her my sincerity and tried to keep the doubting voice inside of me quiet for once. However Miguel translated my answer, it seemed to have pleased Señora Asunción and the boys. I expected applause to break out, but instead Pepe got up and brought over a bottle of wine and four little glasses and poured a finger of wine for each one of us. The Señora did not imbibe.

Before we drank Miguel wanted to finalize the price. Pepe gave a number. By that point I was pretty good at my Spanish numbers, but Pepe had given the price in *duros*, not *pesetas*. I knew from Seville that *un duro* was five *pesetas*, but sitting there without paper or pencil I couldn't calculate the quoted duros into pesetas and then the *pesetas* into dollars to get to the price. Miguel countered with our two-thousand-dollar offer, again in *duros*. Even though I was the buyer, I knew that in Spain this was a male game and I let them play it. Then, just like that, they shook their hands across the table and I was a homeowner. Oh my God! I drank the wine and prayed to all my saints for HELP. Walking back down the hill to where Miguel had parked the car, I tried to picture myself living here in this village in my water-less, electricity-less and straw-filled house that was such a bargain. My gut decided to withhold judgment until further study had been made.

We made it all official-like the next week at the *Notario Público* in Pego. The notary's office was located off a little square at the far end of the main street. I had been a notary once in Washington. I always felt very smug when I was called in to put my seal on a document. When I mentioned that to Miguel, he harrumphed that in Spain a mere secretary could not be a notary. *El notario* was the equivalent of a lawyer (lucky for me that they didn't charge as much as the lawyers I worked for). When we walked in, there was all that male backslapping as the *Notario*, Pepe and Miguel took their seats. But in the end, it all came down to Señora Asunción and me putting our names at the bottom of a very official-looking document. It was really just about us two women—one passing on her hearth and home with the palm-sized key to the next, whom she (and I) hoped was worthy of her memories. We kissed each other on the cheeks, linked arms and walked out alone.

Casa Ana

That was the easy part of becoming the owner of *Casa Ana* at 31 *Calle José Antonio*. (I didn't know then that José Antonio was also a Fascist. It was a few years after democracy officially came back to Spain that those in power replaced all the streets in the country named *Calle José Antonio* with the names of artists, writers, poets or musicians. I think they did it as a way to erase from memory some of the questionable heroes from its Fascist history. My street was renamed *Calle Gabriel Miró* after the Alicante-born writer.) Over the next months I expanded my Spanish vocabulary to include useful words like hammer, nails, plaster, cement and "...but you promised you'd be there today." More importantly, I got to know when and in which bar—there were six in this town of five hundred people—I could find each of the four masons, the plumber, the electrician and the painter on any given day. Sometimes I used my *turista* card, but it only got me into the bar to talk to the workers, not them to my house. So I developed a style of pleading that was somewhere between whining and being one of the boys. I think what finally got them down that steep hill was the realization that I would stop bothering them during their morning breakfast break or when they were having a beer after work if they would just this once finish the wall around the bathroom or put an electric bulb somewhere in the house, *por favor*.

Eventually it all came together—well, longer than eventually, really. I had a lot of direction and gifts from the ladies who lived on my street. Every day one of them would stop by the open door (it was the only way I could see), shake her head and hand me a pot or an egg basket or a discarded chair, but most often it was just advice like, "You shouldn't leave your doors open when the Gypsies are in town." Or my favorite, "This house will fall down on your head one of these days." *Gracias* was all I could say. Señor Asunción never came down. But I heard that she kept abreast of my progress through Magdalena, who ran the grocery store at the top of the street and who knew everything that happened on *Calle José Antonio*. I think the Señora just didn't want to butt in and tell me how things were kept when she lived there. But then one night, just before Christmas, she dropped by unexpectedly. She stepped through the little door and into the painted foyer (I had wanted to keep the calculations on the wall, but the painter thought I was crazy). She took a look at my little kitchen, which now had a working stove and a tiny used refrigerator that some English woman had had in her backyard, rusting away (she still charged me something for it). I invited Señora Asunción into the sitting room where a not-so-bad fire was burning. Then she handed me a bottle of her homemade olive oil and another of that rough red wine I'd drunk at her house with Miguel. She motioned for me to get some glasses and, when we each had a wee bit, she raised her glass to me and said "*Salud.*" Then she grabbed my shoulders and ceremoniously gave me a kiss on each cheek and officially declared that I was now truly the mistress of this house. It made me cry. After the ritual, I escorted Asunción arm-in-arm up the hill to her house. On the way back, I remembered Wayne's map with the X and realized that it really had brought me home.

About the Author:

Ann Eyerman grew up in land-locked Columbus, Ohio. It was the perfect place to nurture dreams of travel and living by the sea. In 1967, when a call came from an old friend offering her a job in Washington, D.C., to work at the Smithsonian Institution, she was on the next Greyhound bus heading east. It was the beginning. Two years later, after a fortuitous lunch, she landed a job at a college in Germany for a year. She didn't say no. That's where she had her first tastes of European life, food, smells, culture, architecture and history. Ann stayed in Europe for almost a decade, writing detailed letters home which, fortunately, her archival-minded mother saved. In 1981, she returned to Washington, D.C., dusted off her typing skills and worked unhappily for a huge law firm, completed a bachelor's degree she had started in 1965 and began her love affair with cats. In 1995 Ann moved to Toronto, Canada. She turned her experience of working in an office in a changing economy into research for a thesis on work and work issues, which resulted in a Master of Environmental Studies and eventually in the publication of *Women in the Office: Transitions in a Global Economy* (Sumach Press, 2000). Ann still lives in Toronto where she works as a job coach, writer, Excellent Cat Sitter and blogger. She lives with two rescued cats, who have become regular contributors to her blog, Annie's Odyssey (http://anneyerman.wordpress.com/).

Made in the USA
Charleston, SC
18 August 2014